D0796237

ADVANCES IN CONTEMPORARY EDUCATIONAL
Jonas F. Soltis, EDITOR

COMMUNITY, DIVERSITY, AND CONFLICT AMONG SCHOOLTEACHERS

The Ties That Blind

BETTY ACHINSTEIN

Teachers College, Columbia University
New York and London

Published by Teachers College Press, 1234 Amsterdam Avenue, New York, NY 10027

Library of Congress Cataloging-in-Publication Data

Achinstein, Betty.
   Community, diversity, and conflict among schoolteachers : the ties that blind / Betty Achinstein ; foreword by Jonas F. Soltis.
      p. cm. — (Advances in contemporary educational thought series)
   Includes bibliographical references and index.
   ISBN 0-8077-4175-2 (cloth : alk. paper) — ISBN 0-8077-4174-4 (pbk. : alk. paper)
      1. Teachers—United States—Attitudes—Case studies.   2. Teachers—Professional relationships—United States—Case studies.   3. School environment—United States— Case studies.   I. Title.   II. Series.

LB1775.2 .A34 2002
37.1—dc21   2001053175

ISBN 0–8077–4174–4 (paper)
ISBN 0–8077–4175–2 (cloth)

Printed on acid-free paper

Manufactured in the United States of America

09   08   07   06   05   04   03   02   8   7   6   5   4   3   2   1

To Chad and Adin,
who have taught me about love and community

Contents

Foreword

We all know that "community" is a soft, warm, and positive term and that "conflict" is a hard, cold, and negative term. In this book Betty Achinstein examines the school reform literature on the desirability of school community building and describes two rich case studies of quite different teacher professional communities in action over time. She deftly uses these real situations to draw a very complex map of the multidimensionality of community and highlights the inevitable role that conflict plays in any school environment. Then, in a very even-handed way, she points out positive and negative potentials of both community and conflict in achieving desirable educational results. She ends with a deep and engaging examination of contemporary communitarian theory as it illuminates the choices educators have in conceiving of and working toward different ends of education in our pluralistic, democratic society.

There is much sophistication and wisdom in this study. It spirals and circles back on itself over and over revealing deeper and deeper levels of meaning and understanding about the concepts of community and conflict, unity and diversity, pluribus and unum, professionalism and the aims of education in a democratic society. This book advances our thoughts about both educational communities and the role of conflict and diversity, but most especially invites educators and reformers to think deeply and make reflective choices about what ends or aims our efforts in school reform should seek to achieve.

Jonas F. Soltis
Series Editor

Acknowledgments

In writing this book, I have had the wonderful opportunity to experience the power of community. Without the community of teachers, colleagues, mentors, friends, and family, this book never would have come to be. I am indebted to the teachers, administrators, and schools that participated in my study. These participants opened up to me and shared their lives and their work, telling stories of both joy and pain. Thanks to their tremendous commitment to education and collaboration, my perspectives on teacher community are enriched. I hope that this work may help other educators in turn.

Some of this research was conducted under the auspices of the Center for Research on the Context of Teaching, Stanford University School of Education. I thank Milbrey McLaughlin, Joan Talbert, and colleagues at the Center for their support and guidance.

I am blessed with tremendous mentors. I can only express here a fraction of the profound experience of working with Larry Cuban. He has been a superb mentor and a rare guide through this journey. I am deeply indebted to him. It was Milbrey McLaughlin whose writing first drew me to this topic. It was her personal and professional commitment to teachers' contexts that helped sustain me through my work. Nel Noddings's work on caring and her critique of the "dark side" of community provoked me to explore conflict and dissent in community. Judith Warren Little's commitment to professional development and her exceptional work on constraints of collaboration have enormously impacted this study. I especially want to thank Jonas Soltis for his excellent feedback and kind words of support. I am also grateful to Brian Ellerbeck and Lori Tate of Teachers College Press for their guidance.

My friends and colleagues have sustained me throughout this process, reminding me of the most important things in life, making me laugh, listening to me, encouraging my work, pushing me to think on new levels, and providing extraordinary support. I am indebted to my critical friends and writing group, including Laura Stokes, Cynthia Coburn, and Tom Meyer. Their feedback and cheerleading sustained me. Thank you to Joel Westheimer for his commitment to community and his role as a mentor. I also want to thank Ellen Moir and my colleagues at The New Teacher Center at UCSC for their support. The STEP+ group of teachers, with whom I have met monthly for 7 years, has kept me passionate and honest about my commitment to practitioners. I thank Kathleen Ferenz and Susan Sandler for opening up their work life to me, and for reading my work and giving honest feedback.

To Katherine and Richard I am indebted for whisking me away and reminding me of joy and laughter. Kelly, Gideon, Bill, and Maggie offered me my home away from home. I thank Brad and Jack, who shared my love for education, talks, and hikes. In particular, Brad Stam provided enormous time and support in my study as he opened doors, read my work, and shaped my thinking. To Ben and Sarah I am thankful for their humor and compassion. Thanks to Laura and Ciara for their laughter and love. Thank you to Cynthia and Nathan, Tom and Julie, and the kids as well. I thank Jenifer, Rowan, Amy, and Richard for their encouragement. Rosalie, Peter, Sarah, William, Lily Rose, and Marcus have always cheered me on.

I want to thank my family for their wonderful support. My grandfather, Asher, guided me with his wisdom and his love surrounded me. I carry on his love of scholarship and commitment to education. My mother offered ongoing encouragement and never let me forget how proud she was. My father's commitment to scholarship and his guidance inspired me. Jon, Lisa, Elizabeth, David, shared words (and pictures) of support. In particular I want to thank my sister, Sharon, and her husband, David, and their son, Benjamin, for providing extraordinary love and guidance. My sister has taught me so much about exploring myself, to learn from this writing journey. From my extended family, Alan, Debbie, Munro and Susan, Ben, Ann, Marcy and Dion, Erin, Gregg, Tim and Kim, Noah and Antonia, Jenifer and Dan, Jesse and Layla, Monique and Sharese, Heather and Alice, and Norah, I have learned about community support. I particularly want to thank Ann Wiener for reading all of my work and offering excellent words of wisdom. Thanks to them all for their enthusiasm. My dog, Emma, deserves recognition because she took me for walks when I was having writing blocks and played ball when I was frustrated.

Finally I want to recognize my husband and son. Adin was born in the midst of writing this book and brought me such joy and a new understanding of a need for community. Chad's love replenished me. He nourished my heart and soul. He bore witness to my pain and shared in my profound joys. He offered me kindness, humor, cheers, compassion, and respect. He journeyed alongside me. I thank you, Chad Raphael.

CHAPTER 1

Community and Conflict Among Teachers

I became a teacher because I was taken with the words of John Dewey, who envisioned schooling as an apprenticeship in democracy, as a sort of greenhouse to enable growth and experimentation with community life. Building this sense of a "life consciously lived in common" (Greene, 1984, pp. 4–5) meant that schools would not just teach about, but would embody community life and promote participation, shared values, and a sense of unity. The goal was not just to reproduce the current society reflected outside of schools, but for schooling to provide fertile ground for improving and transforming society. Notions of unity, social harmony, belonging, and transformation danced through my head. As a teacher I could both create and participate in such a community.

In the early 1990s, I was thrilled to be part of the great democratic experiment that empowered local communities to control their own schools in Chicago. I joined hands with teachers and parents across the city to promote school reform. This was my dream—to grow schools as democratic communities. This initiative also echoed the hopeful research at the time, which advocated building schools as communities and promoted greater collaboration and collegiality among teachers as a mechanism to foster school reform. I was captured by this vision as well when I joined a group of parents and educators in Chicago to found a new public school. We built Thurgood Marshall Middle School on principles of community among students, shared decision-making with parents, and collaborative teaming among teachers. We brought together families and educators from all different racial, cultural, and language backgrounds to form a school as community.

Much to my surprise, I found the reality was quite different. This experiment in community in Chicago was rife with conflict and disagreement. We vociferously debated the implementation of changes. Parents fought with principals, principals fought with staff, and staff fought among themselves and with parents and students over the direction of their communities. Where was the unity promised by community?

At Thurgood Marshall Middle School, I was shocked by the heated clashes over ideology, race, culture, and practices that drew teachers into conflict with one another, mirroring the controversies that arose throughout the city over how to improve schools. On my own grade-level team of teachers who collaborated on a daily basis I found conflict. I remember when Brooke, the only African-American teacher on my team, announced that she wanted all of the African-American girls in her advisory group because "they need me, and I'm sorry, but they won't listen to you." I felt angry not that she found me, a young white woman, unqualified to reach a large population of our students, but that we were unable to discuss the meaning of this. That moment could have been a powerful learning experience had we discussed our own beliefs about fundamental questions of schooling. Yet we left unexplored our own differences and thus any opportunity for growth. We swept that conflict under the rug, afraid to challenge one another especially on such a difficult topic as race and white teachers teaching in a multicultural setting.

THE TIES THAT BLIND

I wrote this book in response to that silence. It is a silence about conflict within schoolwide teacher professional communities, about how to manage our differences while sustaining unity. This book raises questions about how the discussion of community all too often moves from the "ties that bind," an expression of shared vision and practice, to the "ties that blind," an expression that ignores differences and the role of conflict. In this darker expression, the ties of commonness blind us from seeing diversity in community.

Since the late 1980s, a reform surge around "building community" in schools and fostering teacher professional communities has heightened a tension over reconciling differences while attaining unity. As society turns to schools to promote a sense of community while simultaneously calling for recognition of the diversity needed to sustain our democracy, classroom teachers are expected to remedy this intractable dilemma. Yet overly harmonious models of community offered in the research literature often leave practitioners confused and ill-prepared for the conflicts that inevitably arise during their collaboration.

This book reframes notions of conflict within teacher professional communities. While previously considered a dysfunctional or pathological aspect of communities, this volume argues that conflict reflects a more hopeful and healthy future for communities and schools. Conflicts give teachers the opportunity to look at schools as they are and decide what they can become. Conflict, it turns out, offers a context for inquiry, organizational learning, and change. As colleagues air differences, build understanding across perspectives, and seek changes enhanced by divergent thinking, conflict becomes constructive for the community and school.

In an investigation of real teachers' experiences—through their own stories as well as through observation—a picture of what really goes on in schools emerges, which can help clarify the theoretical terms of the debate about unity and diversity. With richly textured case studies of two schools that manage conflict differently, this book shows that when teachers enact collaborative reforms in the name of community, what emerges is often conflict. Whether over teacher collaboration or about how to meet the needs of their diverse student population, conflicts within teacher communities reflect differences in beliefs and practices that significantly affect the school.

This book explores how teacher communities differ dramatically in how they own conflict, practice collaboration and consensus, think about the purposes of schooling in relation to issues of conflict, frame and seek solutions, and utilize mechanisms to manage their differences. Why do we care that communities handle conflict differently? The answer is that different stances toward conflict matter for school reform outcomes. How communities manage conflict shapes teachers' lives, the kinds of bonds and boundaries formed within and without the community, and, most important, schools' capacity for change and learning.

Ultimately, the work examines the kinds of communities we want in schools that reflect democratic goals. Seeing conflict as a cornerstone of democratic process, this book reflects on current social theories of community and democracy to promote values that bind communities but do not blind them to differences.

THE CALL FOR COMMUNITY

Attaining community with diversity is a problem not just for teachers but for our society. We as Americans struggle with sustaining diversity within unity, or maintaining community amid our conflicting interests. We long for a strong sense of community, harking back to a small-town life where face-to-face connections fostered a sense of recognition, obligation, care, and common purposes. Yet we simultaneously recognize that modern life insists that we acknowledge the multiplicity of individual and subgroup differences of identity, values, and interests in our culture. We recognize that our differences make us stronger. But how do we reconcile the two seemingly opposite impulses? "Wholeness incorporating diversity," as John Gardner puts it, may be the ultimate challenge of our time (1991, p. 15).

Gemeinschaft and Gesellschaft

Over 100 years ago, Ferdinand Tönnies (1887/1963) articulated a shift in social relationships away from community-oriented bonds as we moved from traditional to modern industrial society. Tönnies used two terms to explain these changes in orientation. *Gemeinschaft* refers to a strong community based on familial ties or common values. Tönnies refers to three forms of Gemeinschaft relationships: those built on kinship, place, or mind. Kinship offers familial ties, whereas place refers to common geography, and mind refers to bonding around shared values. In Gemeinschaft, mutual obligation, common commitments, and a sense of belonging are strong.

Gesellschaft, in contrast, refers to the public world or society. If in Gemeinschaft people "remain essentially united in spite of all separating factors, in Gesellschaft they are essentially separated in spite of all the uniting factors" (Tönnies, 1887/1963, p. 65). Community values are replaced by contractual ones of modern bureaucratic society. Relationships are more voluntary, goal-focused, and self-oriented. The modern organization offers an example of Gesellschaft relations, where membership is defined through contracts, formalized roles and hierarchies, some common goals, and mutual self-interest.

Today, there has been a resurgence of longing for "community" or ways that Gemeinschaft can reemerge in an increasingly Gesellschaft world. The dangers of individualism; the breakdown of social cohesion; and competition, alienation, and division among social groups seem to loom large and threaten the very fabric of America. A call is heard to rebuild community, to return to a sense of belonging, social interdependence, and harmony. Social critics of modern society have shown how the focus on individualism has neglected and eroded community ties (see Bellah, Madsen, Sullivan, Swidler, & Tipton, 1985; Etzioni, 1993; Gardner, 1991; Putnam, 2000; Sandel, 1982). Modern advocates of community are concerned with an "individualism [that] may have grown cancerous" and thus threatens a communal life (Bellah et al., 1985, p. vii). Some critics challenge liberal social theorists' notions of individualism and competition and offer an alternative vision of interconnectedness, shared values, and an ethic of care (Burack, 1994; Friedman, 1992; MacIntyre, 1981; Sandel, 1982, 1992; Taylor, 1992). Amitai Etzioni (1993), a founder of the modern communitarian movement, has even drafted a "communitarian platform" calling for the promotion of a shared set of core values to unify America, in this way strengthening moral commitment and responsibility to one another.

School and Teacher Communities

With the decline in a sense of community in families and neighborhoods, the public turns to schools as a source of Gemeinschaft development. Beginning in the mid-1980s, educational reformers took up the call for fostering community in schools (Barth, 1990; Carnegie Task Force, 1986; Sergiovanni, 1994; Sizer, 1984). Thomas Sergiovanni (1994) makes the case for shifting the metaphor for schools from formal organizations to community. "Why is community building important in schools?" asks Sergiovanni.

> Community is the tie that binds students and teachers together in special ways, to something more significant than themselves: shared values and ideals. It lifts both teachers and students to higher levels of self-understanding, commitment, and performance. . . . Community can help teachers and students be transformed from a collection of "I's" to a collective "we," thus providing them with a unique and enduring sense of identity, belonging, and place. (p. xiii)

The metaphor of community offers much to schools currently configured as formal organizations breeding feelings of alienation, isolation, and disconnectedness, among students and teachers alike. The image of the urban high school with thousands of students who wander into and out of the classrooms with no sense of connection or relationship; isolated teachers separated by professional hierarchies and balkanized departments, and disempowered by external forces that determine their work; and the lack of common ground or shared values between teachers, parents, and administrators leaves much to be desired.

With the realization that teachers may need to experience community in order to build community with students, reformers have turned their attention to fostering teacher professional communities. The community metaphor for teachers "draws attention to norms and beliefs of practice, collegial relations, shared goals, occasions for collaboration, problems of mutual support and obligation" (McLaughlin, 1993, p. 81). Teacher professional communities are currently promoted through schoolwide reform efforts that foster teacher collaboration and coordination, shared decision-making through site-based management, and team-teaching and peer coaching that enable colleagues to deprivatize their practice.

A focus on the nature of community built among teachers promises shared values and a common vision for schooling, greater collaboration and collective action around school reform, improved teacher practice and student learning, and an ethic of caring and responsibility that permeates the life of teachers and students (Johnson, 1990; Lieberman & Miller, 1984; Louis & Kruse, 1995; McLaughlin & Talbert, 1993; Newmann & Associates,

1996; Noddings, 1992). Community building efforts seek to change the workplace culture from teachers as isolated individuals in an "egg-crate" (Lortie, 1975) structure to a more family-like setting, which promotes collegial work. The metaphor of community was to replace the formal organization or factory model that had made so many schools alienating places for both students and adults.

Community was to be the solution to many of our schools' problems. At the individual level, professional community is seen as a site of support and reassurance from peers, and a way to ease the kinds of isolation and uncertainty inherent in the profession (Cohen, 1990; Johnson, 1990; Rosenholtz, 1989). At the classroom level, community is seen as supporting teaching innovation, risk taking, and effective teaching (Little, 1982; Louis & Kruse, 1995; McLaughlin & Talbert, 1993; Rosenholtz, 1989). At the school level, shared goals fostered in communities enhance the organization's capacity for coordination, teacher empowerment through shared decision-making, and collective achievement of schoolwide reform goals (Barth, 1990; Johnson, 1990; Rosenholtz, 1989; Sergiovanni, 1994; Sizer, 1984). Recent work has also begun to draw connections between teacher professional community and student achievement (Newmann & Associates, 1996).

TOO ROSY A CONCEPTION OF COMMUNITY

I take schools, in common with virtually all other social organizations, to be arenas of struggle; to be riven with actual or potential conflict between members; to be poorly coordinated; to be ideologically diverse. I take it to be essential that if we are to understand the nature of schools as organizations, we must achieve some understanding of these conflicts.

—Ball, 1987, p. 19

While teacher professional community advocates paint a rosy picture, those engaged in practice, like myself, find a different reality—often more complex, diverse, and conflict-filled than the original conception would have us believe. Such optimistic visions often leave practitioners ill-prepared for the dilemmas they will face, or worse, label their attempts failures when they are challenged by complexities. As Stephen Ball (1987) explains in the epigraph above, schools are arenas of struggle, poorly coordinated and ideologically diverse, making conflict not cooperation the norm. Practitioners and theorists need a more complex portrait of teacher collaborative initiatives, which takes into account dilemmas, tensions, and challenges involved in building community.

Naive, Unified, and Uniform Images

Previous conceptions offer a *naive* image, which makes community sound natural and easy to build in schools. Such conceptions ignore the complexities of grafting a collaborative culture onto a teacher workplace marked by isolation, autonomy, and independence. For example, Sergiovanni claims that "once community is offered, we willingly accept it" (1994, p. xvii) and yet from Judith Warren Little's extensive studies, cooperative work among teachers "is scarce, fruitless, or hard to maintain" (Little, 1990b, p. 181). Communities like those advocated by reformers are extremely rare to find in practice and much of what has passed for collegiality has been trivial. Due to strong norms of privacy and autonomy, limited versions of community where teachers engage in "story swapping," rather than extensive "joint work," seem to be the norm (Little, 1990a). An "independent artisan" rather than a collaborator may more accurately fit in teachers' work culture (Huberman, 1993). The very ecology of classroom teaching, the physical layout of isolated classrooms, makes them more "collections of independent cells" than a tightly integrated or interdependent entity (Lortie, 1975).

Naive conceptions also dismiss how state and local administrators manage teachers' work culture. Some forms of community are disguised Gesellschaft relations. These collaborations may amount to "contrived collegiality" where teachers are coopted by leadership to work together for the purposes of others (Hargreaves & Dawe, 1990). The metaphor of community may disguise teachers' real status in a bureaucratic system.

Emphasis on collaboration and empowerment also clashes with the rising trend toward centralization of control over professional standards, curriculum, and school funding. Are teachers members of an autonomous professional community with power or are they laborers dictated to by a larger national context (Hargreaves, 1996)? Creating Gemeinschaft communities within a Gesellschaft and bureaucratic work culture raises many dilemmas (Merz & Furman, 1997). Collapsing Gemeinschaft and Gesellschaft, family and contractual workplace relations, not only conceals the power of the state as employer to manage teachers, but it casts the family as unproblematic.

Advocates of teacher professional community also often paint an overly *uniform* or homogeneous picture of it, which lacks an appreciation of the differences within and between communities, thus minimizing issues of diversity. Characterizations of a unified teacher professional community at a schoolwide level obscure the multiple relevant communities, which are found both within and beyond the school (Little & McLaughlin, 1993). Department and subject-level affiliations, ethnic/racial/language/

cultural identity groups, friendships, professional organizational ties, and multiple and often shifting subgroups form within the larger school context (McLaughlin & Talbert, 1993; Siskin, 1994). Secondary schools are more likely to have balkanized departments, rife with status hierarchies, than a unified schoolwide culture (Hargreaves, 1994; Siskin, 1994). Collaborative reform models that provide a uniform conception of communities can also demonstrate a nostalgia for a homogeneous past, but seldom reflect the diversity and conflict found in either modern schools or society.

Promoters of teacher professional communities would also have us believe they are all alike, yet sharp differences arise between professional communities founded on divergent ideologies, beliefs, and norms. One community may promote social justice while another reinforces the status quo. These different ideologies matter in how schooling is enacted and for what ends.

Past research has also often been overly simplistic in casting a *unified* picture of communities devoid of conflict or rapidly able to achieve consensus (see Barth, 1990; Johnson, 1990; Lieberman, 1995; Newmann & Oliver, 1967; Purkey & Smith, 1983; Rosenholtz, 1989; Sergiovanni, 1994; Sizer, 1984). Conflicts that are recognized are often characterized as aberrant or pathological community behavior leading to fragmentation and destruction rather than a naturally occurring phenomenon, which could foster growth (see, for example, Hartley, 1985; Nias, Southworth, & Yeomans, 1987; Pollard, 1985; Yeomans, 1985; cited in Nias, 1987).

Complicating Community

Another body of literature is emerging with more complex conceptions of teacher professional community, which takes into account tensions involved in building teacher communities that impact school reform and teacher norms and practices. This book joins these critics of overly optimistic conceptualizations of community in the teacher professional community literature and offers a deeper exploration of the complexities and challenges of building and sustaining communities.

This literature includes theoretical and empirical works, some of which offer textured pictures of teachers engaged with struggles of collaboration. For example, Little and McLaughlin (1993) challenge naive and unified conceptions of collaboration by exposing the core tension between teachers' individual, subgroup, and collective autonomy as teachers navigate multiple reference groups. Similarly, Hargreaves (1994) rejects the rosy conception of community with accounts of balkanized teacher collaboration, where subgroups within the school community form cliques that result in negative outcomes for students and teachers. Louis and Kruse's (1995) study of five schools identifies great variability in the development of teacher professional community, distinguishing between mature, developing, fragmented, and static communities. While some communities took collective responsibility for improving student learning and moved forward, others formed communities with only partial participation and high levels of competition among subgroups. Still other communities were unreflective and became "stuck." Challenging the uniform reform rhetoric around community, Westheimer (1998) identifies the vastly different ideologies and practices enacted in the name of teacher professional communities by contrasting two cases. One community emphasized teachers' individual autonomy and rights; the other was defined by a more collective or communal mission and values. Merz and Furman (1997) offer a critique of school reform models that provide a naive conception of homogeneous communities, which do not reflect the complexities of modern society. They further criticize programs that are unnecessarily bureaucratic. They leave the reader with questions about negotiating the dilemmas of creating Gemeinschaft communities within Gesellschaft institutions and society.

While this body of work critiques the rosy picture of community described in the previous section, it rarely explores the dilemma that is at the heart of community: How do members really manage diversity amid unity? How do they negotiate conflict while sustaining community?

CONFLICT IN COMMUNITY

As we have seen, many community advocates and researchers ignore the role of diversity, dissent, and disagreement in community life, and they have undervalued the complexities involved in managing conflicts while maintaining strong communities. They have ignored those very conflicts that could prove vital in fostering school reform and growing strong professional communities, conflicts that mirror the national debates about sustaining unity amid diversity in our democratic and diverse society. While more recent studies have begun to explore the complexities of community, they also leave underexamined the nature and role of conflict amid unity. Finally, the policy and practice enacted from much of the research on community often do not capture the nuances and complexities of sustaining diversity within community.

Communities Arise and Remain in Conflict

Yet, in practice, when teachers collaborate they run headlong into conflicts over beliefs and practices. Teacher professional communities are often born in conflict because they demand substantial change in practice, challenge existing norms of privacy and autonomy, and question existing boundaries between cultures and power groups at school sites (Hargreaves, 1994; Little, 1990a; McLaughlin & Talbert, 1993). For example, Guiton and colleagues (1995) document 12 middle schools that showed how teaming raised tensions between collegial norms and notions of professional autonomy. As colleagues began working more closely together, they challenged traditions of teacher independence.

Communities remain in conflict as their valued norms of consensus and critical reflection, of unity and discord, are oftentimes incompatible. As many have argued, critical reflection is as essential as collaboration to strong communities (Dewey, 1916; Gardner, 1991; Lieberman & McLaughlin, 1992; Newmann, 1994). Critical reflection involves the process of challenging the "taken-for-granted" assumptions of teaching and schooling practices and imagining alternative perspectives for the purposes of changing conditions (Freire, 1983; Louden, 1992; Schön, 1983; Tabachnich & Zeichner, 1991). Such reflection fosters alternative perspectives and growth, and thus serves to counter myopia and stagnation in communities. Yet critical reflection, by uncovering competing interests and questioning existing practices, may result in ongoing conflict. For example, Muncey and McQuillan (1993) describe a faculty split by conflict over notions of reform, restructuring, and decision-making about school goals as they reflected on their change initiatives. Similarly, Louis, Kruse, and Marks (1996) identify addressing students equitably as a source of normative conflicts between teachers as they questioned existing practices around meeting the needs of their diverse student population.

An understanding of conflict within community is thus crucial to practitioners', reformers', and researchers' understanding of how such communities form, cope, and are sustained over time. It is a disservice to those engaged in fostering teacher professional communities to ignore the complexities they will encounter. These teachers need to move beyond the platitudes of "building community" and "respecting differences" to address the reality of the conflicts they face. We need to see real cases of teacher professional community in action, warts and all. This would offer rich and textured portraits of the complexity of enacting what policymakers and researchers advocate. Current depictions of communities without conflict offer an unrealistic picture, inaccurately representing the realities of collaboration in practice. We need an expanded theory of teacher professional community that includes conflict and its relationship to reform outcomes and broader implications for the nature of schooling, examining the critical significance of the role of conflict in transforming conditions for teachers, students, and schools.

Conflict, Reform Outcomes, and Visions of Schooling

The reform outcomes purported to result from building community among teachers are deeply linked to how teachers manage the differences amid their collaboration. My work concentrates on conflict, which I see as the key experience that connects teacher professional community to school change and organizational learning. Communities that can productively engage in conflict have a greater potential for continual growth and renewal. Conflict is a critical factor in understanding what distinguishes a generic professional community of teacher colleagues from a *learning community* engaged in ongoing inquiry and change.

Beyond learning, understanding conflict within community is also central to examining how the educational ideology of such communities shapes the experience of teachers, students, schools, and even society. These ideologies or visions of schooling include orientations about student learning and outcomes, views about teachers' roles, notions about how schools should reform and change, and conceptions of the relationship between school and society. These educational visions frame how teachers view their work and ultimately take action.

There are all kinds of visions of schooling that teacher professional communities may promote. While some teacher professional communities uphold conceptions of schooling for traditional values such as stability and harmony, and the reproduction of current social relations, others may foster more democratic notions of inclusivity, diversity, and transformation of current conditions. In each of these educational visions, conflict plays a different role. In teacher professional communities with a more traditional vision, schools are seen to promote consensus and alignment with dominant values in society. In teacher professional communities with more democratic visions, schooling may play a crucial role in fostering critique in order to transform society.

Current educational literature on teacher professional community lacks a specificity of these educational visions, particularly as they relate to teachers' ideologies about the relationship between school and society, and therefore misses an opportunity to evaluate preferred ends. Communities with vastly different educational ideologies are considered strong and equally positive communities by some advocates as long as these visions are shared within the community.

Exploring conflict as it relates to visions of schooling held by teacher professional communities is especially significant within a democratic system of public schools full of students and teachers of different cultures, beliefs, and abilities. Active engagement in conflict, a dialogue of differences, is a normal and essential dimension of a functioning teacher professional community in a publicly supported schooling system promoting democratic values. We need to understand the complexity of fostering unity within the diversity that makes up our current schools and society. We also must begin to ask what educational visions we want teacher professional communities to have in our schools.

EXAMINING TEACHER PROFESSIONAL COMMUNITY AND CONFLICT

To begin the journey of understanding teacher professional communities' experiences with collaboration and conflict, I offer some working definitions of these concepts. Defining teacher professional communities is complex because of the wide spectrum of teacher-teacher interactions and the multiple affiliations and subgroups identified within schools, and because the types of collaboration or collegiality denoted by the term *community* are conceptually ambiguous.

Understanding Teacher Professional Community

Three kinds of literatures contribute to an understanding of dominant conceptions of teacher professional community found in educational research, policy, and practice: social theory, organizational theory, and research on teachers' work culture. Social theorists and philosophers contribute to a definition of community in society, emphasizing obligations and commitments (see Dewey, 1916; Etzioni, 1993; Selznick, 1992). Organizational theory and change literature identifies institutional configurations of community, articulating the structural and organizational supports for collective cultures and work (see Fullan, 1993; Martin, 1992; Schein, 1985; Van Maanen & Barley, 1984). Research on teachers' work and school culture highlights schools as communities and focuses on relationships among teachers, foregrounding collaboration and shared purposes and values (see Barth, 1990; Little, 1990a; Louis & Kruse, 1995; McLaughlin & Talbert, 1993; Newmann & Associates, 1996; Noddings, 1992; Sergiovanni, 1994).

These literatures highlight three common features. First, as occupational communities, teacher professional communities are engaged in *common work*. They involve a group of people across a school whose identity is drawn from their common work as teachers (Van Maanen & Barley, 1984).

Second, teacher professional communities hold *shared norms, values, and visions* about teachers, students, and schooling. Norms are "the generalized rules governing behavior that specify, in particular, appropriate means for pursuing goals" and values are "the criteria employed in selecting the goals of behavior" (Scott, 1992, p. 16). Vision refers to teachers' orientation and educational ideology about appropriate roles of teachers, students, and schooling. Teacher communities share, to a certain degree, a common vision of how teachers teach, students learn, and schools work.

Third, such communities are organized around *collaborative cultures and structures* that build relationships and interdependence. Avenues for face-to-face interaction, structural conditions that allow for collaboration, and dispositions that foster interconnectedness are found in teacher professional communities. Two sets of scales for measuring teacher professional communities define even more specific criteria of collaborative cultures and structures that prove helpful. McLaughlin and Talbert (1996; Talbert & McLaughlin, 1994) delineate the following criteria: opportunities to learn, collegial support and collaboration, collective problem solving, and a culture of experimentation and innovation. Louis, Kruse, and Marks's (1996) criteria include shared norms and values, reflective dialogue, deprivatization of practice, collective focus on student learning, and collaboration.

Thus, a teacher professional community consists of a group of people across a school who are engaged in common work; share to a certain degree a set of norms, values, and visions about teaching, students, and schooling; and operate collaboratively with structures that foster interdependence.

Understanding Conflict

What, then, is conflict? Conflict is both a situation and an ongoing process in which views and behaviors diverge (or appear to diverge) or are perceived to be to some degree incompatible. That is, conflict can be an event in which individuals or groups clash, exposing divergent beliefs and actions. Conflict can be seen as, "a situation in which the conditions, practices, or goals for the different participants are inherently incompatible" (Smith, 1966, as cited in Rahim, 1986, p. 12).

Conflict is also a process whereby individuals or groups come to sense that there is a difference, problem, or dilemma and thus begin to identify the nature of their differences of belief or action. In this way, conflict is a social-interaction process, whereby individuals or groups come to perceive of themselves at odds. This more dynamic understanding of conflict emphasizes interpretive processes (Kolb & Putnam, 1992). In this view, "There is nothing inherent in the notion of conflict. It is a performance to which different audiences attach meanings . . ." (Felstiner, Abel, & Sarat, 1981, cited in Kolb & Putnam, 1992, p. 13).

It is the process of conflict-definition that I have come to focus on. The interactive states, the socially constructed meanings, the understandings arrived at by individuals and groups about the nature of their differences in beliefs and actions, have been at the center of my work. For example, as teachers came to see a problem around differential treatment of students at one of the schools I studied, they became aware of different beliefs among teachers about how to teach African-American students. Some teachers proposed to pilot a new program. The subsequent debates over program adoption resulted in a conflict event (clashes at the faculty meeting to decide on a proposal). Before, during, and after this event, teachers were engaged in a meaning-making process whereby they were coming to name differences in beliefs and action among teachers in regard to teaching African-American students.

APPROACHES TO AND OUTCOMES OF CONFLICT BETWEEN TEACHERS

To explore how teacher professional communities approach conflicts and what outcomes result from such stances, I draw from my study of two schools as well as the literature on conflict and organizations. I look to micropolitical theorists such as Blase (1991) and Ball (1987) who find schools, just as other social organizations, to be "arenas of struggle" rife with conflict; critical theorists who identify conflict at the center of democratic schooling (Apple, 1990; Freire, 1983; Giroux, 1983); and school change and organizational theorists (Argyris & Schön, 1978; Fullan, 1993; March & Olsen, 1975; Martin, 1992) who highlight reflection, conflict, and change in order to understand organizational learning. I found in my study and these sources four salient dimensions to understanding conflict approaches: (1) conflict ownership; (2) norms and practices of collaboration and consensus; (3) ideology about schooling; and (4) conflict frames, solutions, and mechanisms.

Conflict Approaches

Conflict ownership describes the ways that a community acknowledges or excludes conflicts. It captures how teachers realize that they have differences and come to take responsibility for exploring conflict in their midst. For example, one of the communities I studied tended to acknowledge and at times embrace differences among colleagues. They identified conflicting approaches to addressing the needs of their diverse student population, openly debating different ideologies and practices in order to make changes in their school. In contrast, the other community tended to suppress perceived differences between colleagues, finding ways to transfer problems outside of their community by identifying "outsiders" (e.g., "problem students") as causing the problem or having outside authorities (e.g., the principal) resolve their differences.

I found the nature of conflict ownership to be mediated by the three dimensions of teacher professional community described below.

Norms and practices of collaboration and consensus identify the generalized rules of conduct and structures of teacher-to-teacher interactions articulated by the community. How a community defines its "we-ness" discloses its disposition to difference (those people and beliefs that diverge from perceived community agreements). This dimension also addresses how a community defines and enacts consensus practices (how it comes to collective agreements). For example, one of the teacher professional communities I studied formed a tightly unified body that collaborated on curricular and policy decisions, and also maintained strong personal friendships. Members practiced forms of consensus that tended to diminish dissent in favor of unanimity. Thus they presented a highly united front with little room for divergence.

Ideology defines the framework of shared values about education, schooling, and students held within a teacher professional community. It includes an orientation about student learning and outcomes, views about teachers' roles, notions about how schools should reform and change, and conceptions about the relationship between school and society. Through ideological frameworks, individuals and communities "make sense" of their work and ultimately take action (Ball, 1987).

Ideologies are not solely framed within the teacher community. Both within and beyond the schoolhouse walls, people hold conceptions about the ways schools should be (Cuban, 1984; Meyer & Rowan, 1977). The relationship between the outside- and inside-school ideologies may exacerbate or minimize conflict within the community, as teacher communities align with or clash with beyond-school community values.

I found that one of the communities I studied had a critical ideology of schooling for social justice and transformation that challenged mainstream educational conceptions. This critical stance tended to exacerbate conflict at the school as struggle and challenges to the status quo were seen as central to the purposes of teaching for transformation.

Conflict-frames, solutions, and mechanisms identify how a community defines, makes sense of, and ultimately sorts through options to manage differences. Goffman (1974) explains that we "frame" reality in order to make sense of our everyday lives, negotiate our world, and choose appropriate actions. Frames are the patterns and interpretations used to organize meaning. In the framing of conflicts, communities construct and limit their responses, the range of thinkable thought (Chomsky, 1989), the arena of discourse around an issue, and ultimately the solutions they seek.

One of the teacher communities I studied tended to frame conflicts in singular and manageable ways leading to single solutions. When teachers clashed, they tended to identify psychological or personality differences rather than explore philosophical, pedagogical, political, or other lenses for understanding differences. Thus their solutions to difference often involved removing or separating individuals from one another because of a sense that psychological differences were unchangeable.

Communities may frame conflicts in a multitude of ways. This study focuses on institutional, organizational, and individual conflict-frames. While these three do not encompass all of the conflicts found in teacher professional communities, they were central to how the teachers in my study framed their differences.

Institutional conflicts concern debates about ideology and norms of what and how to teach, what roles teachers play, and what goals are worth striving for in schools. Organizational conflicts involve issues of structure, power, routine, governance, resource allocation, competition, and interest groups. Individual conflicts reflect clashes between participants' social identities and commitments, their personalities, attitudes, and communication styles. Mechanisms to address conflict involve the repertoire of formal and informal procedures and structures to raise and address conflict. These strategies and structures, such as "consensus" procedures, allow for distinct levels of participation in public debate and management of conflicts.

Conflict Outcomes

Ultimately, this book is concerned with the outcomes that result from different conflict approaches. These include changes that may result at the individual, community, or organizational level.

Individual experiences address the impact of conflict on the lives of individual teachers within the community. Conflict may promote feelings of frustration or stress for some individuals. Others may experience satisfaction from resolved differences or deeper understandings of difference. For example, teachers at one of the schools I studied described the increased stress level and sense of frustration caused by continuously raising, without resolving, conflicts about how to best address the needs of their African-American students.

Community ties and borders capture changes to the nature of teacher relationships within and beyond the teacher professional community. Conflict may result in changes around how tightly or loosely the teachers are bound together. It may also result in delineating the borders of a community. Borders identify the extensiveness or inclusivity of the community: Is it schoolwide or departmentalized? Does it extend into other communities beyond the teachers or even the schoolhouse walls? For example, as the result of the conflict stance of one of the communities I studied, teachers who disagreed with the majority left the school. Teachers who remained at the school felt closely tied to one another by their common beliefs and were able to delineate clear borders of their community by excluding dissenters.

Organizational change involves shifts in structures, reform efforts, and norms or practices at the whole-school level. For example, as a result of a conflict among teachers about meeting the needs of their students of color at one of the schools, the teacher professional community initiated a schoolwide reform effort and an extensive inquiry process focused on equity. This enabled organizational learning around issues of equity at the school.

Organizational change is a particularly significant outcome given claims of advocates that teacher community fosters a potential for fundamental change, reculturing, ongoing renewal, and learning at the schoolwide level. Organizations can "make meaning" and "learn" from past events (March & Olsen, 1975) by adapting or transforming norms and practices.

It is important to note, though, that there are different kinds of learning, some that tend to maintain the stability and status quo of the organization versus those that result in ongoing inquiry and fundamental change. For example, faced with a similar conflict about meeting the needs of diverse students, the other teacher community learned to maintain their current practices in the face of a conflict about not meeting the needs of their diverse students by transferring a conflict onto parents outside of the teachers' perceived locus of control.

Learning that results in reactive, adaptive, or superficial changes, transferring knowledge for future decisions (Levitt & March, 1988; March & Olsen, 1975), and identifying and correcting errors (Argyris & Schön, 1978) falls into the status-quo categorization. Here, an organization seeks to adjust to its environment while maintaining core norms and practices. In contrast, learning that results in generating new insight to change behavior (Huber, 1991) and routinely questioning values that guide organizations (Rait, 1995) falls into the ongoing inquiry and fundamental change category (Scribner, Cockrell, Cockrell, & Valentine, 1999).

THE STUDY

This book examines two schoolwide teacher professional communities located in urban public middle schools in the San Francisco Bay Area that are engaged in schoolwide collaborative reform initiatives. The study explores how each community approached conflicts between teachers and what outcomes resulted.

The Schools

I chose two sites—Washington Middle School and Cesar Chavez Middle School (both pseudonyms)—that self-identified and were recognized by outside agencies as strong professional communities distinguished by their collaborative reform efforts.

Through further study, I also found that they measured as strong communities on scales identified by researchers on teacher professional community. Both schools exhibited shared norms and values, common work and visions, and collaborative culture and structures. Further, both scored as strong communities by scales developed in terms of opportunities to learn, collegial support and collaboration, collective problem solving, and culture of experimentation and innovation (McLaughlin & Talbert, 1996; Talbert & McLaughlin, 1994). Finally, both met Louis and Kruse's (1995) criteria of shared norms and values, reflective dialogue, deprivatization of practice, collective focus on student learning, and collaboration.

With their explicit focus on supporting collaboration, challenging traditional boundaries of secondary schools' departmental divisions, and collaboration-focused state reform initiatives, California middle schools are important sites for both community and conflict. They were also actively involved in regional and/or national reform initiatives focused on collaboration. I also chose urban sites that reflected the kind of cultural diversity that can give rise to conflicts among teachers.

In many ways the schools are similar. Both have racially diverse populations of about 600 African-American, Latino, Asian, Filipino, and White students. The middle-school philosophy of interdisciplinary teaming, collaborative teacher planning time, and engagement in restructuring efforts is similar at both sites. And yet, the schools are cases in contrast. While one teacher professional community sustained its personal and professional ties by suppressing differences and marginalizing dissent, the other embraced conflict as the center of its work. Each approach resulted in vastly different kinds of communities and schools.

Washington Middle School stands atop a hill in a lower-middle- and working-class neighborhood of ethnic and racial minorities. The 29 teachers form a homogeneous group of primarily White women who do not live in the community where they teach. The staff is close personally and professionally, sharing views about schooling that promote socializing culturally diverse students into society. The second school, Cesar Chavez Middle School, stands like a tower on a hill, next to a fenced-in blacktop playground. Students come from low-income and racial-minority communities and are bused into a middle-class neighborhood. This 42-member staff is racially and culturally mixed, includes both men and women, and represents a diversity of teaching styles and beliefs. These teachers espouse values about schooling for social justice and social transformation.

A Case Study Approach

I chose a case study approach using ethnographic techniques that emphasize richly contextualized data to get at often hidden processes. A case study approach offers an opportunity to capture an in-depth description of teachers engaged in collaborative initiatives, their experiences with community and conflict, and the impact on individuals, communities, and schools. This approach also contributes to theory-building.

Although this is a case study and not an ethnography, I used ethnographic methods, which prioritize the insiders' views and construction of meaning. For this study, the insiders' perspectives were essential to capture the multiple meanings that individuals and groups constructed to make sense of conflict. Conversely, an external perspective provided the theoretical and analytical lens from the outside, setting the insiders' views in context. My approach required stepping beyond the insiders' reported experience, adding another dimension to the discourse on conflict.

In this case study, I combined both qualitative and quantitative methods. The qualitative work enabled studying conflict as a process, teachers' interpretation of meaning, and my participant observer role in the fieldwork and analysis. The quantitative work, in the form of a survey, enabled both corroboration and new lines of thinking (Rossman & Wilson, 1991).

While I conducted research at one school site for over 4 years between 1994 and 1998 (intensively examining conflict over 2 academic years), I studied the second site intensively for only 1 academic year (1996–1997). I spent extensive time in staffrooms and classrooms trying to observe teachers in the midst of collaboration and engaged in conflict. I collected data through four primary means: ongoing interviews with approximately 50 teachers and administrators; observations of formal and informal meetings and interactions; document analysis of current and archival documents; and a teacher survey adapted from McLaughlin and Talbert (1996).

At each school I chose a subgroup of seven target teachers, which comprised an eighth-grade-level team with which to conduct a more intensive series of interviews and observations. The tape-recorded semi-structured interviews included questions about the nature of teacher professional community, the schools' approaches to conflict, and reflections on critical incidents that occurred during the study. I observed both formal and informal meetings 1 to 4 days a week at each of the sites. I also spent time in such informal settings as staffrooms, copy areas, restrooms, classrooms, schoolyards, and faculty social gatherings. I collected a variety of documents, including reform proposals, meeting agendas and minutes, and vision and mission statements. I distributed a survey to the whole faculty at each school addressing conflict within teacher communities and teachers' work culture (see Appendix for further methodological discussion).

There were some important ethical considerations involved in doing a study on conflict in schools. I maintained strict confidentiality to avoid exacerbating conflicts or disrupting the teacher community. This work required sensitive judgment and a sympathetic ear to respect individuals and the larger community. My goal was to understand more about the processes of conflict, not to cause it. I came to this topic as a former teacher who understood well the experience of conflict within community.

Since I have begun working on the topic of conflict in communities, I have been called on to address practitioners on the topic. I am often filled with both excitement and dread at those moments, for the work that I have done here does not translate into a recipe for other schools to manage conflict. Case study research can generalize to theory, not populations (Yin, 1989). While there are important lessons to be drawn that are applicable to communities with similar contexts, some cautions remain. The schools with which I chose to work were uncommon. They were highly innovative schools with self-described strong teacher professional communities. Both were small and engaged in multiple reforms. Although there are some important implications about the nature of teachers' relationships with students, I focused primarily on the teacher professional community, venturing less into the experience of students. Finally, I captured only a snapshot in the life history of two teacher professional communities, not following the patterns or cycles of conflict approaches over a longer period of time.

Yet, examining richly contextualized case studies of teacher professional communities engaged deeply in the work of collaboration and conflict has much to offer toward a conceptualization of teacher community for researchers and practitioners alike. It is through the examination of real teachers' lives that we can come to see the complexities of fostering unity amid diversity, and begin to unravel some of the promises and dilemmas engendered by the resurgence of a call for community for teachers and schools.

PREVIEW OF CHAPTERS

Chapter 2, "Washington Middle School," tells the story of a highly unified homogeneous teacher professional community defined by norms of caring and interdependence. The staff of primarily White women were proud of and relied on their close-knit personal and professional ties. These relationships made conflict a particular challenge. Conflict with colleagues hurts both "the heart and the head," said one teacher. Washington's was a community that often sustained its unity and organizational stability (limiting change) by achieving rapid public consensus, privatizing differences, or transferring disagreement outside its borders.

Chapter 3, "Chavez Middle School," examines the struggle within a teacher professional community. The racially and gender-diverse staff shared critical ideological values about educating for social change and thus welcomed conflict and dissent. At Chavez, the teachers acknowledged and critically reflected on their differences of belief and practice in efforts to foster fundamental change in the school. The teachers embraced conflict as central to the purposes of their community. While such a stance toward conflict fostered organizational change and diversity within unity, it took its toll as teachers experienced frustration, stress, and turnover.

Chapter 4, "Conflict Amid Community," compares and contrasts the two communities and the conflicts they faced. By using examples from each school, I offer contributions to understanding the complexities of communities' relationship to conflict. The analysis reveals an unexpected marriage between community and conflict. Collaboration and consensus actually generated conflicts as teachers made public their divergent beliefs and practices. Using the contrasting cases, I develop a spectrum of conflict approaches and outcomes along which the two schools lie. I argue that a conflict-embracing, rather than conflict-avoidant, stance offers a greater potential for ongoing organizational learning and renewal. I conclude with reflections and implications for the theory and practice of teacher professional communities.

Chapter 5, "Beyond the Ties That Blind," asks what educational visions held by teacher professional communities we want for schools. Which visions are preferred given the context of our public schools and democratic society? I explore a spectrum of teachers' visions of schooling in order to examine and evaluate these ends. This final chapter returns to a philosophical dilemma at the center of initiatives to foster community in school—how to support wholeness incorporating diversity.

CHAPTER 2

Washington Middle School

"$C = (D \times V \times F) > R$" written on butcher-block paper greeted Washington Middle School teachers as they entered their first meeting of the year. As the 29 members of the faculty sat at long tables formed into a square at the center of the library, they chatted about summer activities and preparation for the new school year. After introducing Kate, the one teacher new to the school, the principal turned to Sophie, an eighth-grade team coordinator and language arts teacher, for an "inspirational moment."[1] Sophie stood in the center and explained what she had learned at a change-management summer institute. Pointing to the butcher-block paper with lettering, Sophie said:

> We need to see what we are dissatisfied with at our school. The D stands for dissatisfied. The V stands for vision. The F for first steps. These three things all must be greater than any resistance (the R). If any of these factors are zero, then change (the C) won't work. Most schools don't look at dissatisfaction. . . . So the point is we need to get messy. We do talk about our problems, but we do avoid some problems.

Balancing this equation was a challenge for Washington teachers. Talking about their problems, especially ones that seemed to threaten their shared norms and close ties, was a complex undertaking.

The Washington teachers who listened to their colleague formed a tightly knit community of like-minded practitioners. It seemed like a family reunion as they gathered in the large teachers' lounge after the meeting to share lunch and catch up on each other's lives. Each teacher had a cubby for his or her coffee mugs. Notes about "Thank God It's Friday" gatherings and a teacher book club, the monthly calendar of meetings, and a thank-you message for those who brought in food for teams on "Tuesday Treats" days were written on the white board next to a microwave and a coffeemaker. Photos of teachers and their families were bound in a staff album displayed prominently at the central table. The room looked well lived in, colorful with announcements and pictures. It was the lively center of activity throughout the year as teachers met there to eat, plan, gossip, debate, and generally take refuge from students.

After lunch, grade-level interdisciplinary teams met. The "Champions" team, a group of four women and one man (along with one teacher's baby), met around a small table to plan their first interdisciplinary team unit. They had worked together for years and it showed. They finished each other's sentences and referred to curriculum ideas in the secret code only teachers who have taught closely together know. Joking and handing around the baby, the team prepared for its first day of classes.

One of the team members, Karen, described her relationship to colleagues.

> These are my professional friends. We collaborate and we like each other. I think there is a unique and strong sense of collaboration among actually all my staff. . . . [It is a] loving, warm, extremely close collaboration.

But such close ties at Washington also made conflict a difficult matter to examine among adults. Karen, a social studies teacher, explained, "Team collegiality is better for teaching, worse for conflict, because it's personal. It's your friends." Sophie said that close ties made conflict between the teachers rare and difficult because it would rupture both personal and professional relations. Sara, another eighth-grade team member and a math teacher, agreed:

> I've never worked in a place with such close friends. . . . When conflict happens, it's not a head thing, it's a heart thing. . . . It becomes a conflict in my soul. I'm emotionally involved in the conflict. I do care and it really hurts.

THE SCHOOL

Washington Middle School is an urban public school of 650 seventh- and eighth-grade students located in the San Francisco Bay Area. Standing atop a hill in a lower-middle- and working-class neighborhood comprised mainly of ethnic and racial minorities, the school is a collection of rectangular flat buildings and outdoor corridors. The student population is highly diverse: 37% Latino, 26% Filipino, 12% Asian, 12% White, 9% African-American, 3% Pacific Islander, and 1% Native American. About two-thirds of the students are immigrants or first-generation citizens. Sixty percent speak a native language other than English. Over the past 10 years, White students have decreased by about 10%, while Latinos have increased by about the same percentage (Washington Report Card).

Washington is one of 15 schools (12 elementary and 3 middle) in its district of 8,000 students. About 15 years ago, teachers struck over salary. The district administrators restructured 10 years ago, decentralizing and giving school sites more control over their budgets and greater resources. Further, more stakeholder input was solicited from parents, businesses, and universities in the community. District officials supported reform efforts at Washington through grants, recognition awards, and increased professional development. Administrators also exerted pressure on the school to improve on district- and state-mandated standardized testing.

Ted, the principal, a White male, joined Washington 12 years ago. He was committed to school restructuring and engaged the school in applying for grants to support middle-school innovations in interdisciplinary team teaching and collaboration. Washington School is a leadership school in the Bay Area School Reform Collaborative (BASRC), a regional reform initiative that focuses on supporting schools to take on comprehensive, student-focused, whole-school change processes, as well as engage in regionwide change. BASRC encourages and funds schools to undertake a "cycle of inquiry," whereby practitioners pose questions, collect and examine data, and determine actions for reform. Further, the school has been noted as a "California Distinguished School" and a "California League of Middle Schools Visitation Site," identifying the school as a model site for achievement by the state.

Engaged in restructuring efforts, the school has emphasized teacher teaming and interdependent work, consensus-based decision-making, schoolwide standards, and high expectations for all students. Washington's recent reforms focused on aligning the scope and sequence of its curriculum with one of its five feeder elementary schools. The faculty of both schools met twice monthly with local university facilitators to develop coherent or "seamless" curriculum and standards across schools.

TEACHER COMMUNITY AT WASHINGTON

Washington's teachers are highly homogeneous. The staff of 29 is predominantly White and female, with two teachers of color and six men. Laura, a seventh-grade teacher, explained, "We're all White females. That's what [the principal] calls us, 'a White women's school.'" The predominance of White teachers stands in stark contrast to the diverse student demographics. All but one teacher live outside of the community in which they work. Almost all of the faculty have been at the school for more than 5 years and some teachers (at least five) have been at Washington for over 20 years. Teacher turnover is low. The principal reported that one to two teachers leave a year.

Collaborative Practices

Washington teachers collaborate at multiple levels: Interdisciplinary teams plan integrated curriculum units, subject-matter departments agree on common performance standards, and schoolwide decisions involve the whole school in reform efforts. The staff at Washington began a process of restructuring in 1989 that resulted in organizing four interdisciplinary teams, two at the eighth-grade level and two at the seventh-grade level. Each team consists of teachers in science, math, language arts, social studies, and "enrichment" (art, computer, etc.). The teams meet on Tuesday mornings and are accountable for producing portfolios of their interdependent work each year. Students come in later on Tuesday mornings, so that teachers can meet.

Teachers exhibited a high level of interdependence in developing integrated curriculum and planning schoolwide activities. One eighth-grade team of teachers organized every curriculum unit interdisciplinarily and knew what each expected from students, what lessons were taught when, what skills were covered, and the success of each unit. Their students created "products," such as books about leadership, that represented all of the subject areas. Teachers collaborated in helping plan each other's lessons, including strategies to reach "English as a Second Language" (ESL) students. They discussed the students they shared in common and planned team-level events. Shannon, a seventh-grade teacher, explained the power of cooperation in the following way:

> The teams, I think, make a big difference in [how] teachers are working together because it does away with that isolation that teachers have had for so many years. I can see that more and more teachers are much more open about what they're doing and willing to talk about it. I think for years, you'd just go in your room and close the door and you didn't talk about anything. Especially on this grade level. . . . But now with the teams, we are more into each other's curriculum. We like to share things about what we are doing and see how it fits into what the other person is doing.

The teacher meeting schedule (see Table 2.1) depicts the multiple levels of collaboration and the amount of time spent in teams at Washington. Each of the grade-level teams developed a name (such as the "Champions") and met for 90 minutes every Tuesday morning. These teams formed the core of teacher collaboration. Subject-matter teams also met up to once a

TABLE 2.1. *Washington Teacher Meeting Schedule, 1996–1997*

MONDAY	TUESDAY	WEDNESDAY	THURSDAY	FRIDAY	SATURDAY
Leadership Team Meetings (monthly) 3:15–5:00	Grade-level Team Meetings (weekly) 8:26–10:00	Department Meetings (monthly) 3:15–5:00	Parent Teacher Student Association (monthly) 6:30–8:00		Professional development associated with BASRC grant in collaboration with local elementary school (monthly, sometimes not on Saturdays but during the week) 8:30–3:30
		Faculty Meetings (bimonthly) 3:15–5:00			
		School Site Council Meetings (monthly) 3:15–5:00			
		BASRC Leadership Team (bimonthly) 3:30–6:30			

month to plan schoolwide standards and coordinate curriculum. The faculty met as a whole every other week to make organizational decisions and shape student programs. Other groups met to govern the school, such as the Leadership Team and the School Site Council, which met monthly. The Leadership Team, composed of teacher leaders and the principal, met to plan faculty meetings and define schoolwide change proposals. The Parent Teacher Student Association also filled out the schedule. Finally, Washington's reform work associated with its BASRC membership called for a joint team with a local elementary school for professional development and coordination.

According to survey data, the faculty strongly identified itself as a "teacher learning community" (with a mean score of 4.08 on a 5-point scale).[2] On items where they could strongly disagree (value of 1) to strongly agree (value of 5) with statements, teachers at Washington reported a great deal of cooperative effort among colleagues (4.14) and a low degree of isolation (1.75). They strongly agreed that they were continually learning and seeking new ideas from each other (4.17); that they regularly met to discuss common problems and challenges in the classroom (4.39); and that they critically reflected together about the challenges and successes of the school (4.14).

There was a strong sense of unity among colleagues, who identified themselves as being part of a whole-school community (3.96). Kristi, a physical education teacher at Washington, described her colleagues as a "community of friends," who were "as tight as can be." A close social network of personal and professional relationships reinforced the teacher community at Washington. From the "Sunshine Committee," which coordinated social events for teachers, to the close personal friendships throughout the school, one noticed a special bond between teachers at Washington. There was a sense of congeniality, of laughter and tears shared, of strong and caring ties among the teachers. The personal friendships among colleagues involved grade-level teams eating lunch together in the faculty lounge, weekly walks on the school premises, "T.G.I.F." celebrations, vacationing together, sharing baby stories, and even passing one teacher's baby around during meetings.

Teachers described their connections to their colleagues as caring relationships. Karen, in the eighth-grade team, described these bonds as a "loving, warm, close collaboration." Jackie, a staff member, described the importance of the faculty to her:

> [They] mean more than I can explain. I lost my husband two and a half years ago . . . and the support that I got from everybody is something that I will never forget. I do love my job.

Such close personal and professional ties translated into a level of expressed trust and support among colleagues (3.50).

Ideological Stance

Washington's teacher community can be said to hold a common ideology or framework of educational values as reflected in their mission statement, common work with students, and conversations. Washington teachers reported that they shared beliefs and values about the central mission of the school (3.86). Many described the faculty as "like-minded" and having the "same educational values." Washington teachers shared a common commitment to their school reform agenda. All teachers at the school agreed to participate in BASRC professional development obligations that involved over 90 additional hours of work for the year (although over time, one teacher did not continue with the extra meetings after school). A school document, written by staff members for the purposes of gaining funding from BASRC, recorded that "there are no opposers to the [reform] vision" (Washington Addendum to the Action Plan, BASRC).

Washington teachers' shared ideology can be characterized as mainstream in their alignment with dominant local and national public conceptions of schooling. This ideology involved socializing students into our current society and promoting a conception that equal opportunities were open for all to advance based on ability. In contrast to a more critical interpretation of education that would see the role of schooling in transforming the society, Washington teachers saw their role as educators to help socialize students to be productive members of society. Their vision statement explains, "We envision a school that empowers students to become productive and responsible members of our richly diverse community and to give service to our community" (Washington School Vision Statement).

Such values were present in Washington's reform agenda. Karen, a social studies teacher, described the staff's conception of reform in the following way: "It's not about changing society. It's about bringing these students' scores up." Washington's reform focus was to align the curriculum to meet school standards and improve student achievement as measured by traditional tests.

> Our hypothesis is that the creation of a coherent, articulated, K–8 curriculum will enable all students to be successful learners and communicators. We believe students, who are actively engaged in a coherent curriculum which is meaningfully connected to their lives and interests, will develop the skills and habits of mind necessary to succeed academically. Success will be measured by the number of students who meet the grade level benchmarks and the 8th grade standards. Traditional measurement, CTBS scores and grade analysis, will also be used. The expectation is that all students who participate for all nine years in our curriculum will significantly outperform a matched control group which do not receive our curriculum. (BASRC funding application, p. 6)

Here, teachers disclosed their assumptions about the power of schooling to improve the individual, and their conception of achievement based on effort.

CONFLICTS AT WASHINGTON

Ellen: There are horror stories of our faculty at incredible odds.
Dan: It used to be that way.
Val: But people like each other here now.
Ellen: An approach has been implanted so we don't see that conflict. [The principal] uses the term *consensus*.
Dan: Yeah, we took those who disagreed and shot them. (Laughter)

Val: That's true. They are not here. If you are not going to conform, you are going to leave. The precedent has been set up that those unwilling to do that will not be here. (Conversation among eighth-grade teachers in the Washington faculty lounge)

While Washington teachers formed a close community, they also experienced conflict. The responses to each conflict encountered were remarkably similar: The teachers sought ways to avoid conflict and quickly resolve their disagreements or transfer them to those deemed "outsiders" in order to reclaim unity within their community. As the exchange above discloses, the faculty removed "resisters" in efforts to maintain "consensus" and ultimately, as Ellen explains, "an approach has been implanted so [they] don't see . . . conflict."

Overview of Conflicts

While it was often difficult to see the conflicts because of the norm of avoidance, conflicts still arose among colleagues at Washington. Conflicts about teacher collaboration and those about student concerns captured two broad categories of teacher disputes at the school.

Schoolwide conflict arose when a collaborative reform initiative was first introduced 10 years earlier. Inter-team conflict developed as teams competed for resources. Further, intra-team conflict emerged as individual teachers remained "resistant" to collaboration or experienced "personality differences" among team members.

Conflicts about student concerns involved disagreements over approaches to disciplining "problem students." Furthermore, a problem arose about the "30%" of the student population who were not meeting academic or behavioral standards and what to do with them. Finally, teachers debated inclusion of special education students in mainstream classes.

There was a recognizable pattern in the teachers' response to these conflicts. The teachers tended to identify an "us/them" dichotomy, which situated conflict outside of their community, thus reinforcing a sense of unity within. They developed strategies to transfer their conflicts to others (such as administrators) to resolve or outside of their own domain (identifying students as the problem), thus enabling little change within the community. At times, teachers left conflict hidden or suppressed in order to maintain a sense of unanimity and solidarity among colleagues. (See Figure 2.1 for a summary of conflict types, approaches, and outcomes at Washington.)

By examining in greater detail some specific instances of conflict about collaboration and about student concerns, we can see the recurring themes of avoidance and transference. The next section explores each type of con-

FIGURE 2.1. *Conflict Types, Approaches, and Outcomes at Washington*

TYPE OF CONFLICT	APPROACHES	OUTCOMES
Conflicts about Collaboration:		
Schoolwide		
Conflict over introduction of teaming reform (10 yrs. earlier).	Confrontational meetings about reform. Administrators intervene and resisters marginalized.	Resisters gone. Interdisciplinary teams in place engaged in tightly interdependent work.
Inter-team		
Competition between grade-level teams over resources such as technology and money for special education students; lack of communication and sense of jealousy between teams; special education team feels marginalized.	Competition and jealousy discussed only in private conversations.	Ongoing inter-team competition and jealousy. Continual exclusion of special education team.
Intra-team		
Individual teacher seen as not collaborating or resistant to collaboration.	Teacher threatens group with union. Facilitator goes to principal. Group unhappy with "outsider" in their midst.	Principal intervenes. "Outlier" teacher still seen as outsider but less resistant. Teachers still frustrated privately.
"Personality" differences on teams related to different attitudes toward students and teaching.	Complaints about different "styles." Teacher goes to principal to suggest switching team membership.	Principal reorganizes teams, switches team members to align "personalities."
Conflicts about Students:		
Discipline		
Conflict over lack of discipline and administrative support for discipline. Concern about "problem students."	Faculty discusses frustrations and need for more discipline. Faculty meets with police. Informal meeting of 15 teachers discusses fears and frustrations. Times when teachers raise alternative approaches, conversation closed down with "are we going to support our own (teachers against the students)?"	Call for tougher discipline. More referrals and suspension of students.

FIGURE 2.1. *Cont.*

TYPE OF CONFLICT	APPROACHES	OUTCOMES
Reaching Certain Student Populations		
Concern about "30%" of at-risk students who are not meeting academic or behavioral standards; what to do with them. Conflict between school's vision statement that all students can learn and teachers' practices of labeling problem students and excluding them.	"Hidden" conflict not discussed or only in private. Frustration discussed in team meetings, refer certain students to counseling, negative labeling of certain students in full faculty meeting. Some discussion of finding alternative places for them. High level of frustration among teachers.	Refer certain students to counseling. Hope that BASRC curriculum work will help. General frustration. Seek ways to exclude certain students from school activities and classrooms.
Conflicts over inclusion of special education students in mainstream classes. Debate among special education teachers about inclusion philosophy.	Private concerns about special education inclusion. One team discusses conflict about placing certain students in regular classroom—seen as personal issue between special ed. teacher and regular ed. teacher.	Frustration with special ed. Tension between teachers over spec. ed. inclusion. Removal of certain special education students from some mainstreamed classrooms. One special ed. teacher eventually leaves school.

flict, highlighting a vignette that details this recurring stance. The incidents described below in more detail were chosen because they were representative of the conflict responses exhibited in most other conflicts at Washington during the course of my study, and expose dominant patterns in relation to managing conflict within the teacher professional community.

Conflicts About Collaboration

Conflict about collaboration was generated both when interdisciplinary teaming was first introduced as a school reform and as the faculty implemented teaming over time. At its inception and throughout the lifetime of collaborative reform work at the school, community building created conflicts.

Introducing Schoolwide Collaborative Reform. Interdisciplinary collaboration was first introduced in 1989 by the principal and a core group of three teachers who piloted a single interdisciplinary team. By the end of the year, faculty meetings were called to expand the collaborative initiative. Many faculty members identified emotionally charged confrontations at these faculty meetings between those labeled "resisters" and the "reformers."[3] Multiple teachers remarked that when the restructuring reform was initiated, individuals resisted because of their fear of change and lack of commitment. Some described teachers opposed to the teaming reform in psychological terms, as having "emotional problems." One of the original innovators, Shannon, a seventh-grade teacher and chair of the Leadership Team, recalled, "We had some real dramatic faculty meetings with people yelling and just saying they were not going to do this and they are not going to change . . . or do anything different."

Administrators from the county office intervened, introducing consensus-based decision-making procedures to the faculty. Many teachers identified the consensus process as important in learning skills to deal with the conflict. Bert, a physical education teacher, reflecting the broad sentiment of others, defined consensus as when "everyone agrees." Some stated that consensus helped the faculty feel like everyone wins, rather than the win-lose perspective of voting. There was, however, some confusion about the practice of consensus decision-making versus voting. In some faculty meetings the teachers found out what the majority wished and called that consensus.

While consensus processes were identified as important in handling this conflict about the school reform initiative, teachers said the conflict really ended when resisters left, or, as Shannon recalls, they "retired, or they went or moved." Many faculty members described a general sense of relief at these departures. Ted, the principal, captured some of this sentiment:

> There was a younger faculty member who was extremely volatile and he left on his own volition. He was a resister in the classic sense. He had some emotional problems . . . and there were a few others with more traditional kinds of concerns and they kind of all left. . . . I remember one teacher who was retiring came up and gave this fiery speech about all the things we fought for in the past with our strike and you're willing to work for the planning period for this [little amount of] money. She gave this impassioned speech and then she retired and everyone said, "Thank God."

By 1991 every teacher had become affiliated with a team with common planning time and the conflict was considered "resolved." The outcome was public consensus among the remaining teachers about teaming. Such consensus was achieved through exclusion of those seen as resisters.

As I interviewed staff in 1996–1997 about their current state of collaboration, I heard much agreement that teaming had positively transformed the climate at Washington, bringing a sense of unity. Jackie, a staff member, concluded:

> When I first came we were not into the interdisciplinary teams. . . . There was a lot of bickering between teachers. I've seen over the past 7 years, the whole school—teachers, classified, everybody who works here—come together to work as one unit. The best thing that I feel that ever could have happened was the interdisciplinary teams. They're all very compatible.

This sense of unity was also reported in a case study of teaming at Washington written by two teachers at the school, who conducted a survey and a series of interviews in 1995. They found that "teachers felt that our interdisciplinary teams had a positive impact on our work environment" (Morgan & Rizzo, 1995, p. 8). In particular, teachers valued the increased interaction among themselves.

In the midst of overwhelmingly positive teacher responses to collaboration, and a sense of a whole-school community, I heard only a few voices that privately voiced a different response. In an unusual interview, Eliza, a special education teacher, remarked about the problem of labeling resisters and the impermeable boundaries formed within the school. She was a teacher in a marginalized department (representing the often labeled and marginalized special education student population) who often saw things differently than the rest of the faculty.

> The staff feels that they really do have the right to judge people, flat out. That person is a resister, that person is a reformer, that person is in with the assistant principal, that person is in with the principal. People stay within those roles and they're defined by these roles. At least that's what I have seen. And they very rarely break out of them.

Eliza decided to leave the school at the end of my year of study there. She explained to me that she didn't feel that the principal and the school supported the special education program and her work. She would feel more comfortable elsewhere.

Inter-team Conflicts. While Washington teachers weathered a conflict over the introduction of teaming, they continued to face disputes over collaboration. The inter-team conflicts were often identified as competition or jealousy between grade-level or disciplinary teams, and were usually discussed in private conversations within a team. These conflicts were often connected to issues of power and prestige over access to resources. They represented the micro-political negotiations of the teacher community in which certain teams formed a core while others remained on the margins. The special education and physical education departments were especially marginalized in conflicts over resources and power. Rarely raised in a public setting, these feelings of exclusion were identified within a team or by an individual in an interview.

These teachers fit awkwardly into the academic core interdisciplinary grade-level teams, as they worked with students across grades. They could be found wandering in and out of Tuesday morning grade-level meetings to go to other teams to make announcements or to meet together as a department. In budget debates, both departments were concerned that, with the focus on the core academic grade-level teams, they would not be prioritized as important and therefore not receive the proper support.

Since they were expected to meet in grade-level interdisciplinary teams while still teaching multi-grades, carrying a heavier student load, without the appropriate budgets, both physical and special education teachers often felt "less than" other teams. In particular, the special education teachers were unclear whether they even had department status, having no chair and no budget. It was assumed that special education students benefited from the expenditures of the grade-level teams even when most special education students were not mainstreamed and thus would not receive the benefits. Special education teachers said they were working without enough resources and with outdated materials (like texts from the 1960s). Further, the special education teachers felt that the staff as a whole had not addressed a larger issue of their beliefs and practices about mainstreaming special education students. While some teachers supported inclusion, other teachers would "return" mainstreamed special education students to special education teachers, claiming they were not ready for their classrooms.

Intra-team Conflicts. Beyond whole-school and inter-team conflicts, teachers also experienced intra-team conflicts about teacher collaboration. The 1995 teacher research study conducted by two Washington teachers reported that teachers at their school found individual personality differences to be a root source of these conflicts within teams. Using the metaphor of marriage, teachers identified interpersonal problems in collaboration.

> Teachers were careful to point out that along with all of this collaboration and communication, there is often a good deal of conflict with individual teammates. Edna likened the teams to a sort of four person marriage: "Team members are 'married' for an entire year (or two years). Interpersonal conflicts can become difficult." (Morgan & Rizzo, 1995, p. 9)

Some conflicts within teams that were identified as personality or style differences were "resolved" by the principal intervening and switching team membership. Differences within a team were seen as a problem to be fixed. The solution was to seek the external authority of the principal and reorganize organizationally rather than to address underlying differences between teachers.

The members of the Champions eighth-grade team were four women and one man who had worked together for 3 years or more (Pam and Karen had teamed together for 10 years). Sophie taught language arts, Karen taught social studies, Sara taught math, Pam taught technology, and Dan taught science. The four women were personal and professional friends, socializing after school, even vacationing with each other, and going to workshops together. The fifth member, Dan, had been in the district for 26 years but joined this team 3 years previously, after being moved from another team by the principal.

The team had a reputation at the school for being at the forefront of effective teaming, developing innovative curriculum, and involving the use of technology in their work. As I observed, these teachers were able to finish each other's sentences, rapidly came to agreement on curriculum and pedagogy practices, and shared a common history of working closely together.

Though this team exhibited great unity (personally and professionally), the Champions also experienced intra-team conflict. New or different members posed a problem. Sara described the difficulty of her first year at Washington "breaking in" to the tight social network of the Champions team.

> When I came on the team I definitely felt like a fifth wheel—not really into it. So I felt like I had to really work hard for them in order to prove myself, that I could be a part of this team. . . . They were very tight. . . . It was really hard in the beginning. . . . I'm feeling really left out, I don't feel a part of the team.

After proving herself as a "team player" by showing her willingness to do interdisciplinary curriculum, and approaching another colleague privately about her feelings of social exclusion, the new teacher began to feel more included in the team. She too became tightly tied both professionally and personally to the team.

A "Resistant Teacher." The story of a "resistant teacher" exemplifies both the kinds of conflicts that arose at Washington and the typical response exhibited within the professional community. I highlight this example, which demonstrates how those who challenge the dominant practices and beliefs are often labeled resistant and are marginalized within the community.

Dan, a relative newcomer to this team and the only male, challenged the collaboration expected by his colleagues and became identified as a "resister" to teaming.

At the first Champions team meeting of the year, the teachers planned the first interdisciplinary unit, which was on "leadership and the election." The team sat around a table strewn with materials, calendars, and planning books. Sara passed her baby to a colleague and they cooed over him. As the first four teachers explained how their curriculum would contribute to the common theme for the fall, the fifth was less talkative and struggled to fit his science activities into the interdisciplinary plans.

Then Sara explained that she would be working on polling. Karen told her, "There's a ton of stuff on-line I can just print out. Kids can take the Gallup poll." Sophie explained about the essays she would be having students write on leadership. When asked what he would like to do, Dan asked, "Are you asking what I want to cover in science? Or what you want me to do here?" The team facilitator, Sophie, responded, "What you want to do for the first month." He replied, "atoms, molecules, and heat." Sophie's jaw dropped as she saw a failure to connect with the team's interdisciplinary "leadership" theme.

After further discussion of the activity he did last year in relation to a similar unit, he agreed to adopt the same focus on "leadership qualities that we look for in a president." The team moved on. At the end of the meeting Dan left, and the other four remained. Sara said, "He wasn't so bad." Another team member turned to me and said, "You can see who is the problem in the team."

Sophie, as teacher facilitator, explained the history of Dan's experiences on the team.

> The first year he was really resistant and pretty much we didn't team with him at all. Last year he got a little bit better and he's seeming a lot better this year. . . . The first year he pretty much would do his own lesson plans and stuff during team meetings. He never asked any questions. He never had any input with what you were doing. . . . He pretty much was not going to tie in.

Dan explained his experience on the team that first year.

> I probably didn't contribute very much. Number one, I didn't know how. Number two, I didn't feel safe in it. You didn't know what certain people were going to say to you. . . . So that didn't make it very easy.

He also explained some subject-matter concerns that may have limited his collaboration on interdisciplinary teaming, saying, "I don't think this team realizes how much time it takes away from a science curriculum to do some of these projects."

Team members privately expressed their frustrations with his behavior around collaboration. They would share their thoughts in each other's rooms when he was absent or talk to me about it in interviews. Sara described her discomfort with meetings when the group was responding to the resistant teacher.

> There were some really tense meetings. I was just sitting there going, "Oh, my god, I don't want to be here." We would all leave in horrible moods because of little blowouts. And a lot of it dealt with [him]. He didn't want to team or he didn't understand what we wanted. He went against the group.

The science teacher also felt excluded, claiming he was ignored even when he attempted to collaborate, and had become frustrated with the team.

The conflict accelerated 1 year ago, when Dan said that he would call the union if he was continually pressured to team. He said he objected to teaming because of "the huge amount of time that's involved, above and beyond what we are already required to do." He also felt they had not evaluated the effectiveness of their teaming work. So much time involved with little pay contributed, he felt, to "deprofessionalizing teachers."

Dan connected the teaming conflict with a threat to teachers' professionalism and hard-won union gains. Recalling the contract they had won after the teachers' strike some years back, he continued:

> So they really go outside the contract to do this [teaming reform], which means that you don't know from one year to the next if the contract is really valid for you, or can the majority of your teachers [at your school] change your working hours, wages and working conditions?

He took a question to the union lawyer (American Federation of Teachers) about contracted time to collaborate. Dan explained that the union lawyer said that if "the school votes by majority to do it, you have to do it even if it's not in the contract." This was one of the rare references to unions in the course of my study at either school. It is striking that the teacher communities' identity as professional colleagues may have superseded their union membership. Further discussion on unions will be taken up later in this book.

Sophie, facilitating the group at that time, described her feelings about the conflict.

> [He was saying,] "I'm not staying after school. That's not contract time. I don't have to." He was going to bring the union in against me. I was like, "You know what? We just won't team with you. I don't really have to do this. I'm not getting paid extra to try and convince you that it's worthwhile." It was pretty ugly for awhile.

Sophie was concerned about a "threat to call the union on me" and she approached the principal, asking him to hold teachers "accountable for participating" in teaming. The principal spoke with Dan, identifying his obligations to the team. Ultimately, the principal intervened with this teacher, enforcing his participation in team planning and collaboration.

The rest of the team recognized some changes in Dan after his meeting with the principal. They said that he made more attempts to coordinate his curriculum. Dan remarked that in his third year with the team, "I'm more relaxed. I'm more open. I'm more willing to say this doesn't work for me and even give different ideas of how to do certain things." Karen said, "He's come a long way, he really has, but there's this underlying thing. . . . He's just on a different time frame than we are."

Throughout the year I observed the team, Dan spoke the least in meetings, was often interrupted, and was still seen as an outsider (both socially and professionally). Dan was involved in interdisciplinary units, contributing to final products. Periodically other teachers showed surprise that he did participate in activities such as field trips. But the other teachers remained frustrated with the level of teaming exhibited by Dan and still considered him a resister.

Conflicts About Student Concerns

Beyond teacher collaboration, Washington teachers also experienced conflicts over students. In particular, debates arose about how best to address students who were perceived as behavioral and academic challenges. Teachers discussed what to do with these "problematic" students.

Vision versus Practice About "All Students." The school's published vision statement emphasized the faculty's belief that "all students can learn." Teachers also reported that there was a common agreement among themselves about high expectations for all students (3.89). As part of their restructuring efforts, the Washington staff developed commonly agreed on high performance standards for students in all subject areas.

But many teachers expressed other sentiments. In at least six different formal faculty meetings, the teachers and principal publicly referred to certain students or groups of students, who were perceived as academic and behavioral challenges, as "problem children," "unreachable," "dysfunctional," and "driving us crazy."

Teachers discussed in faculty meetings how low student motivation was "spreading like a contagion." Moreover, teachers identified growing problems with student disruptions in classrooms, including students swearing at teachers, defying teachers' orders to go to the office, breaking school property, and getting out of their seats and disrupting the class.

"The 30%." Teachers referred to 20–30% of the students as "the problem"—defined as those "at risk." In the 1995 self-study written by two Washington teachers, the report referred to "the 30%" as the label given to those students who were not succeeding either academically or behaviorally (Morgan & Rizzo, 1995, p. 17). "The 30%" was common lingo at the school. These students received two or more Ds and Fs, or three or more "Ns" for "not-acceptable" behavior, or were put on the schoolwide "Nonparticipation list" and were thus excluded from all student-sponsored activities. Listed students were referred to as the "non." The assistant principal, Dave, explained that about 80 students (13% of the school) were currently on the non and "very few get off it once they get on."

Some teachers concluded that these students should go elsewhere. One reported, "The 30% need alternative kinds of schooling. I don't think a regular school can deal with them" (Morgan & Rizzo, 1995, p. 20). Most advocated tougher disciplinary measures, more counseling, and referrals to special education.

To add to the challenges of addressing at-risk students, bilingual and some special education students were mainstreamed. Most teachers expressed frustration at the challenges of integrating bilingual and mainstreamed special education students into their classrooms. Eliza, a special education teacher, during her first week of school, said two teachers told her that this school would be a great school if it weren't for the "damn special ed. kids." Some regular education teachers had special education students removed from their classrooms because they saw them as too much of a disturbance. Some teachers found the ESL students a challenge in holding equal standards for all students.

These discussions of problem students and the 30% often collapsed poor academic performance, behavioral problems, and challenges of special education and bilingual integration into one category. During the course of one team meeting when teachers were identifying students for special services, the team facilitator asked the teachers to "jot down 10 names of kids who are driving you crazy, who you think need extra help." One teacher asked her to define "driving you crazy." She responded, "At-risk." When the teachers continued to discuss at-risk students to label them for special services, one member asked, "What's your definition of 'at-risk?' I think we need to go by a definition." The facilitator, Sophie, responded:

> I think "at-risk" is just a general category. I think "at-risk" can be either academic or behavioral. I don't think it has a really clear definition. I think sometimes the behavior is getting in the way of academics and academics are sometimes getting in the way of behavior.

Pam described her ESL students: "They are not driving me crazy other than I don't have the skills to reach them."

Teachers expressed enormous frustration with students they deemed "unreachable." Karen declared at a team meeting, "I've been teaching for 10 years and I've never seen it like this." Others, such as Eli on the seventh-grade team, described, at a faculty meeting, "hitting the wall." In an eighth-grade team document, some teachers explained that they have begun to focus their attention on the "reachables." At an eighth-grade team meeting, Karen said:

> We have 80% of the kids who are willing to work and we have a huge 20% who are so desperately needy they just suck up the energy. I'm not sure whether to move forward or not because I can't keep the kids who can't function. . . . Despite all this, I really want to service the kids who want to learn and at some point I let go of the other kids as long as they don't bug the rest.

At team meetings, teachers addressed particularly disruptive students whom they had identified as hindering the other students who wanted to be in class. While the team planned ways to "isolate" them, Pam explained to the teachers the need for "cutting this rotten spot out so the rest of the apple can survive."

Students Identified as the Source of the Problem. While a few teachers privately acknowledged a sense of not serving all of the students, others, in more public forums, saw the issue as a problem that resided within the students. Sara explained:

> We don't feel that hard core bad students are getting what they should get. . . . Some kids just won't get any better. It's a parental

issue. It's a home thing. We can't go any further. The parents don't care. The kids need help that is psychological. It's not my job. I can't help a kid with a horrible home life.

Similarly, Sophie identified the root as psychological conditioning that teachers could not address.

It's just kids who I think have given up. I don't think it's our fault. It's some sort of not experiencing success along the way. I think it's just they're used to failure. [They think,] "I don't know how to do it. I didn't know how to do it last year." I think it's a lot of self-esteem. You could do some self-esteem activity; it's not going to help. It's some sort of conditioning. And probably a lot of it has to do with home and then not succeeding in school and they're just trucking through.

Faculty reported that colleagues saw student failure as caused by student background and family (3.67). Marie, an eighth-grade teacher, explained the cultural difference between some parents' expectations and those of the schools:

Their parents are not involved. And it's not putting the blame on it, it's just that in some of the cultures they're coming from their parents don't know how the system works here. The system where they're from is different or they're just not sure. There's a different emphasis in the culture where they come from. Their expectation of what the school does and what the home does is different.

Some teachers faulted the administration for not supporting strong discipline because these "kids need tight boundaries," or understanding the "changing students at Washington" (Morgan & Rizzo, 1995, p. 14).

Teachers' Role in the Conflict. Only in the privacy of their team meetings or individual interviews did I hear a few teachers raise the idea about teachers' role in this conflict. Eliza identified teachers' shortcomings in addressing certain students, "But our population is 30% at risk. . . . We are still not reaching a significant part of our population." In a discussion in a special education meeting, Eliza disclosed teachers' "blaming" approach to dealing with difficult students.

When [the 30%] is talked about as a faculty, I perceive there are a lot of people laying blame rather than looking for change. . . . When I have brought it up in meetings . . . what I get back is that "you have to understand the population we are dealing with. These parents don't communicate with their kids. The kids don't communicate with their parents. They don't have parental support. So there is nothing we can do. So why even bother trying to deal with it?"

In private, the same teacher identified teachers' role in the conflict about students in the following way:

I think that every time we say things like, "look at their background; look where they're coming from; look at their home life; look at their parents; we can't help this kid because their parents are this way or we can't help the kids because their sisters are this way," I don't know that it's so much associated with race per se. I think race plays a small part of it. But I think that goes back to [the fact that] we just don't know how to talk to those Black kids.

These are very brief moments of including themselves as sources of conflicts over students. For the most part, individualizing, psychologizing, and pathologizing the students framed the conflict. The comment above was one of the rare references to race that I heard all year at this school, and one of the few instances of teacher identification of disagreement among colleagues in ways to address student concerns.

A "Problem Student." The story of a "problem student" exemplifies both the kinds of conflicts that arose at Washington and the typical response exhibited within the professional community. I highlight this example to demonstrate how teachers transferred conflicts to "outsiders" and sought to exclude them in ways that sustained unity and stability within the teacher community. Further, the story exposes how a conflict that could have surfaced about teachers' stated goals that "all students can learn" and their practices of excluding certain "problem students" remained hidden.

The agenda for the November 13th faculty meeting included the following item: "discipline issues—those students for whom defiance is a lifestyle." The specific incident in question involved Lani, an African-American eighth-grade student, and the faculty's attempts to remove her from the school.

Karen, on the eighth-grade team, described an incident in which Lani confronted her and refused to go to the office. She reported that "the student reacted violently and aggressively toward me." As described in Karen's letter documenting the incident to the administration, Lani was reported to have waved her hands in the teacher's face in a "threatening manner." Karen explained that she was "backed against a wall and closed my classroom door to protect the rest of the students. The girl kept pounding on my door." The principal and assistant principal came to take Lani to the office, but she continued to argue. Lani was suspended for 5 days.

Karen was extremely upset and shared her concerns with other teachers. Other faculty members were similarly concerned about Lani's behavior, and the disciplinary actions that followed. Heated discussions about the incident arose both in the lunchroom and at faculty meetings.

The principal had called in a local police officer to the faculty meeting to clarify that what this student did was not considered an "assault" and thus Karen could not file criminal charges. Most teachers who spoke up at the meeting wanted Lani expelled or to have stronger disciplinary or legal action taken. At the faculty meeting, Shannon, a seventh-grade teacher and facilitator of the Leadership Team, said, "You can't punish a person forever for their act. Even murderers get out in several years. Five days is the maximum days allowed. The child needs another place to go. We don't know what to do with her."

The subsequent faculty discussion included comments such as one from Ellen, an eighth-grade teacher: "We need alternative classes for some of the social misfits." Some teachers raised concerns about the other students in the class who had witnessed this aggression against a teacher and were "the victims," that is, made to feel unsafe in their own school. The principal, Ted, concluded the topic by saying, "The vast majority of our kids work hard, but every team has some for whom defiance is a life-style."

Months later, on March 5th, another student discipline issue arose regarding the same student and teacher. At the end of a faculty meeting, 15 teachers remained after school for 2 hours to discuss the problem. Their discussion moved from this specific incident to disruptive students in general. Maria, an eighth-grade teacher, said to the group, "You send them out because you can't deal with them and they're infecting everybody else." This medical metaphor of disease was heard again when teachers identified negative student behavior as spreading from one bad student to another; "it's infectious" and "it's growing."

Discussion turned to stronger disciplinary measures, more administrative support for discipline, and a more effective discipline committee. When some teachers began to focus attention on adult responsibility for different approaches to teaching or adult interactions with students, others quickly turned the focus back on students.

Karen began to explore the issue as not "discipline," but rather an issue of students' emotional needs that teachers had failed to meet. She suggested a focus on developing an affective component connected to their schoolwide academic reform efforts. Karen explained, "What if we did the same kind of work that we did here academically, we looked at the affective part?" Others responded that it was a problem with the students, not one that teachers could address by changing teaching styles. As Sara put it:

> But we've done all this work on the academics. We busted our asses and still there are kids who sit in my room and do nothing and turn nothing in. There are always going to be that core because their parents obviously don't care. The kids don't care. So I feel like we are going to have this hard core of kids who are going to try to do their best to disrupt things.

Another teacher also moved the focus to the adults' responsibilities to students, hoping to explore some avenues for more professional development in reaching them. She explained that maybe the teachers should re-think their own practices and develop new strategies to avoid escalating student discipline problems. Comments quickly turned back to identify the problem within the children. Pam explained, "I don't think I need any tips on discipline. I think I handle it pretty well. But I'm telling you that I do need help with kids that have been allowed to grow into monsters, absolute monsters."

Teachers also channeled the conflict outside of their own group by faulting school and district administrators. Teachers were frustrated with school site disciplinarians for not reinforcing teachers' expectations for student behavior. Others, like Laura, a seventh-grade teacher, called for unity within the school and identified the problem outside at the district level. "Everybody in this school, I think we're all in this together. I think it's a bigger issue. . . . I'd rather blame [the superintendent] and the board than the administration of the school."

Teachers disclosed a strong sense of concern for their colleagues. Pam showed solidarity with Karen, the teacher involved directly in the conflict with the student, saying, "I'll tell you that personally when I see a friend, somebody that I consider to be a fine teacher, sitting out in the parking lot crying, it breaks my heart and it makes me wonder what this is all about."

At the end of this discussion, teachers zeroed in on the problem as rooted in certain students who needed to be isolated from others or re-moved from the school. Cora, a seventh-grade teacher, said, "We need to have special places for these kids. They don't belong here. But there is no special place for them." Ellen, an eighth-grade teacher, said, "The [U.S.] President said, 'isolate those kids.'" The group then moved to strengthen-ing existing policy, and developing stronger disciplinary actions. As Pam asked, "Are we really willing to suspend and expel people?" Cora called for solidarity among teachers. "Aren't we going to support our own?"

CONFLICT APPROACHES

How can we make sense of the case of Washington teacher professional community? This section explores the approaches to and outcomes that resulted from conflicts within their community. I found at Washington a community that quickly resolved, transferred, or avoided conflicts in order to sustain its unity. It is a case of strong ties that bind and at times blind the community to conflict in its midst.

Conflict Ownership

It was difficult at first to find conflict among teachers at Washington. On a survey, some teachers stated: "I'm not aware of any teacher conflicts"; "As far as conflicts between teachers, I know of none"; "Not aware of any! I've had none myself"; and "Can't think of any conflict among teachers that I noticed" (Achinstein, 1997). Washington teachers tended to move conflict to the margins of their community through excluding it or transferring their differences onto others.

Washington's teacher community avoided conflict by excluding dissent. At Washington, those teachers who were resistant when the teaming reform was first introduced left the school. As Dan jokingly said, "We took those who disagreed and shot them." Val confirmed, "That's true. They are not here. If you are not going to conform, you are going to leave." This was also the case when Dan questioned teaming and remained an "outsider" within the team. Similarly, Eliza, the outspoken special education teacher critical of some of Washington's teacher practices, eventually left the school.

Beyond marginalizing dissent, Washington teachers transferred responsibility or ownership of conflict to those outside of their community. They often handed over to the principal responsibility for conflict resolution. When the Champions team struggled with Dan's challenges, the teacher facilitator went to the principal for support. When differences arose among teachers in other teams, teachers went to the principal, who intervened to switch team membership. Teachers deferred to an outside authority, thus diminishing conflict ownership within the community.

Washington teachers also often constructed an "us" versus "them" dichotomy in their conflicts, channeling or ascribing internal conflicts to external sources. In this way teachers found a common outside enemy such as resistant teachers, problem students, and parents as a way to squelch internal conflict. Thus some conflicts, such as the episode with Lani, were identified as a problem with students (between teachers and students) rather than a conflict among colleagues about teachers' practices of addressing students' needs. Such transference served to foster a sense of solidarity and unity within the teacher community, a sense of "supporting our own."

While there was a discrepancy between the school's vision statement about student expectations and teachers' public discourse about problem students, it was defined outside of teachers' collective debates and transferred to students. The conflict over the negative labeling of students or alternative ways of addressing "the 30%," which might have challenged teacher unity, remained unexamined or avoided.

Instead, the conflict focused on naming problem students as "other." The language of disease and metaphors of contagion, including such terms as "infecting everyone else," were ways of constructing students as the problem. Such medical metaphors suggested the need to quarantine or surgically remove deviants to save the life of the organism. Thus teachers discussed ways to "isolate those kids" or expel them. This approach tended to blame outsiders for the conflict, while leaving internal norms and practices within the teacher community unchallenged. Ultimately, such transference left unexamined teachers' responsibility for 30% of their students.

Norms and Practices of Collaboration and Consensus

Washington teachers' practices of collaboration and consensus reinforced their conflict-avoidant stance. Their enactment of collaboration, which involved close-knit ties that bound teachers both personally and professionally, made conflict a challenge of both the heart and the head. Conflicts were described as painful experiences for teachers, who perceived of themselves as a community of "friends." Beyond friendship, many described in a survey their collaborative relationships with colleagues using the metaphor of a marriage (Achinstein, 1997). Karen, an eighth-grade teacher, explained the challenge of conflict at a school where ties are powerful and teachers' personal and professional commitments are intertwined.

> School is your life and so you can't break away sometimes and be just a hard-ass professional, especially since for us the team has gotten to be very collegial and loving as well. Which is better for the teaching, but worse for the conflict . . . because it's personal. It's your friends. You're having to deal with the affective side.

Demographic homogeneity also contributed to a bonded community that diminished dissent. The perception that "we're all White women" within this community added to the sense of consensus and agreement among colleagues, and a lack of conflict. Although two teachers of color were at the school, the issue of racial difference among teachers, or between students and staff, was rarely raised.

The teachers' conception of consensus also served to diminish conflict in favor of a perceived "unanimity." The circumstances surrounding the introduction of consensus decision-making at Washington reinforced a conception of consensus as a way to end conflicts, achieving total agreement with no dissent. A trainer from the county office taught the faculty consensus decision-making as a way to address conflicts and debates that had arisen about the collaborative reform initiative. In the end, dissenters were labeled "resisters," and most left the school, reinforcing the perceived unanimity of the remaining teachers.

The push toward unanimity was powerful at Washington. While teachers reported that consensus was achieved, it often took the form of dissenters deferring to a majority. When asked, "How does the staff deal with those that disagree with the majority decisions?" Laura, an eighth-grade teacher, responded, "I'm sure they do get kind of bowled over. I'm sure they really feel that way. I feel like we just proceed, in spite of them. . . . There's a lot of peer pressure here." Seventh-grade teacher, Toni, explained the process as "deferring to the majority":

> I think the faculty is really very cohesive. Again, it's a diverse group
> of people and they don't certainly all feel the same way about
> things, but people sort of defer to the majority most of the time.

Bert, a physical education teacher, reported to me a time that he did object, during a debate over a restructuring initiative to create longer blocks of class time and to move to a five-period day. He explained the consensus process:

> Well, the majority of the faculty thought it was best to go to a five-
> period day. [My objection] was talked about but that was about it.
> [We came to] consensus, not a vote. Consensus means that every-
> body agrees. If you have someone who disagrees, then there's no
> consensus. [In this case,] I abstained. I just didn't vote. That means
> that I accepted the reasons why we were doing it, even though I
> didn't agree.

Bert understood that consensus was when everyone agreed. There was, though, not a place for a dissenter like himself. He stated that he had to "abstain" from the process. He also expressed that he was not satisfied with the outcome of the decision: "I believe that it came about for the overall faculty—yeah. For myself, no. It's what the faculty wanted, it's what the majority of the faculty wanted."

Interestingly, while trying to distinguish consensus processes from voting (a process that allows for majority rule), Bert still collapses the two processes, explaining, "I just didn't vote." There was sometimes confusion about what consensus decision-making meant in practice at the school (when to use it and when consensus had been achieved). In at least two cases I observed of consensus decision-making during faculty meetings, the staff demonstrated confusion between voting and consensus procedures. They often found out what the majority wanted and called that a consensus.

Ideology

The teachers' shared ideology of schooling also served to marginalize conflicts. Their shared framework of values identified schools as sites for socializing students into our current society. Teachers' roles were thus to maintain the status quo. Such a consensus-oriented conception served to maintain social equilibrium and stability within the school (Apple, 1990). The alignment between the vision of schooling held by those within the school and that of the local and national community further encouraged harmony rather than conflict in the school.

This is not to say that the faculty was uninterested in reform within the bounds of the current system. They were engaged in reform efforts that served to align their curriculum with their feeder elementary school, to foster interdisciplinary teaching, and to support improved student achievement. These, though, in no way challenge a vision of our society as it is now. Rather than change society, the teachers focused on raising students' test scores.

Conflict and exploring differences in professional beliefs and practice were thus viewed as negatives that would undermine the purposes of the school. For example, differences in beliefs about practice exposed within one team resulted in switching team members. The solution was to reorganize organizationally rather than to address underlying conflicts. Diversity in opinions was seen as a deficit and difference, a problem to be fixed.

Similarly, teachers who challenged the majority and "brought about conflict" were considered "problematic." Oftentimes they were undermined using psychological terms, as when Ted, the principal, characterized a dissenting teacher as someone who was resistant, volatile, and had emotional problems.

Self-reports of Conflict "Ownership"

While I found the teachers conflict-avoidant, Washington teachers tended to report on surveys that they "embrace" more than "avoid" conflicts (Achinstein, 1997). Further, when teachers were asked how they dealt with conflict between colleagues; teachers referred to their ability to "talk through problems" or "hash things out" (Achinstein, 1997). Teachers tended to report that when they disagree, they openly discuss differences and that they do a good job of talking through diverse opinions and values in the school.[4]

If the community found itself successful at embracing conflict, what does that mean? Is it that they could easily resolve conflicts quickly through suppressing differences? Or is it that they prize their relationships most and a "successful" approach to conflict is one that leaves ties intact? Thus whether the substantive content of the conflict was addressed or not, the fact that individuals "get along" in the end seems to demonstrate success to teachers. In this view, "embracing" conflict means embracing relationships with colleagues.

But what *kinds* of conflict were embraced and what kinds were not? That is, did Washington teachers easily embrace conflicts over resources or personality differences between teachers while avoiding institutional conflicts over failing to reach 30% of their students? Did the teacher community have more difficulty publicly addressing conflicts that threatened the ties between teachers, or their conception of themselves as a community with strong common agreements? The answers lie in the community's conflict-framing and its mechanisms to address disputes.

Conflict-frames, Solutions, and Mechanisms

Washington teachers often defined conflicts as problems with one clear cause and ultimately a single-best solution. The clarity and consensus around the public problem framing were notable. For example, while there may have been alternative ways of defining conflicts about student concerns, the teachers almost unanimously identified the problem as within the child. Instead, it could have been framed as a racial and class issue (all middle-class White teachers and all low-income students of color), or a reform issue about addressing affective needs of students, or a parent-outreach issue.

Teachers identified "individual" sources behind most conflicts, attributing them to interpersonal, individual differences, and offering psychological explanations. This, in turn, was reinforced by their conception of themselves as a community of friends with strong informal networks for addressing conflict. Thus, the community viewed conflicts through a relational frame.

At times, this framing constrained the community's ability to address other ways of seeing conflicts. When the eighth-grade science teacher criticized teaming, the other teachers saw it as his psychological deficit, rather than opening a discussion about limitations of teaming or concerns about autonomy, time management, contract obligations, or subject-matter integrity.

Similarly, teachers identified the root of "problem children" as a psychological phenomenon of home conditioning that teachers could not address. The faculty conversation that began to surface about different beliefs about discipline and teaching that could have provided an occasion to reconsider practices was cut short by continually finding the root of the problem in a child's or a parent's deficit. By blaming students for the problem, schools and teachers were not responsible for changing any practices.

When conflicts were not framed as individual problems, they were most often identified as organizational ones. Here, conflicts were seen as problems of resource allocation, procedural complications, missed communication, and poor planning. When individual teachers had different beliefs about teaching and learning, the problem was viewed as one of organization and the solution was to shift team membership.

Washington had some mechanisms for addressing conflict publicly, but their circumscribed repertoire for public debate often reduced deliberation to technical problem solving of organizational concerns. Less often were institutional conflicts about norms, goals, and values raised or addressed in this setting. In their discussion of disciplining "defiant" students, the faculty approached the subject as a procedural clarification by the administration and a police officer (both outside the teacher community), rather than an open discussion about how to approach these students differently.

In contrast, active informal strategies for addressing conflict often served to privatize and personalize differences. These private disputes may have perpetuated a perception that conflict talk was considered "unprofessional" or not worthy of public and therefore professional debate. Networks of friends communicating over lunch or behind closed classroom doors served to mediate differences. Many teachers were involved in "reconnaissance" missions to remedy differences between teachers, going from individual teacher to teacher behind closed doors. These informal settings were seen—as Shannon, a seventh-grade teacher, stated—as "less confrontational" than a public setting. Laura, also teaching seventh grade, explained how conflict was handled "underground":

This is one of the things that you talk about at lunch if somebody is not there or you talk about with your friends if somebody is not there. If the issue gets brought up in a meeting, people might be hesitant to say anything or then people . . . might feel like everybody is picking on them. It's something that's all underground.

Because many of the conflicts that teachers identified were seen as "personality differences," informal settings seemed appropriate. But some conflicts that might have been considered normative debates over differences in educational goals and values were defined as personality clashes and relegated to the private sphere.

Deferring to the principal as final arbiter of conflicts was also a mechanism for resolving differences, removing the conflict from public debate among the teacher community. The principal played a significant role in the Washington professional community's experience with conflict. "I'm conflict-avoidant," he proclaimed. His goal was to smooth over tensions. When team members disagreed, the principal switched teachers. When the eighth-grade teacher challenged his teaming obligation, the principal again was involved. In the conflict about a problem student, the principal contacted the local police officer to come in and define "assault" to the teachers. In all these cases, the teacher community was able to look to an external authority to address and resolve differences.

In a private interview, the principal, Ted, disclosed that he knew he should take a role in initiating a schoolwide discussion about how the teachers were or were not addressing the needs of their diverse students. But he said that he would wait for a year or two before raising these potentially conflict-producing issues because he did not want to threaten the collaborative work on curricular reform that was already under way. He thus identified his leadership role as carefully orchestrating what and how conflicts would be brought to the faculty, and disclosed his sense that conflicts could be easily managed in a rational way (introduced at a specific time and place when people would be ready). Finally, his own conflict stance and his wish not to disturb collaboration and reform echoed and informed the conflict-avoidant stance of the teacher community.

Ultimately, Washington teachers' conflict-framing, solution-seeking, and conflict-managing mechanisms help explain the discrepant results found in survey reports. As Washington teachers framed conflicts in singular ways, they rapidly agreed on both the problems and the solutions. Not exposing deep normative or value differences allowed teachers to maintain close relationships throughout conflicts. In this sense, the teachers were able to "absorb" conflict and reintegrate as a community. Thus, teachers reported in the survey a capacity to "embrace" conflicts and a high level of satisfaction with conflict resolution. However, their framing limited the array of issues that could be addressed, and thus I argue that Washington teachers "excluded" or at times "transferred" other normative or institutional aspects of their conflicts.

CONFLICT OUTCOMES

These conflict approaches characteristic of the faculty and principal influenced individual, community, and schoolwide outcomes at Washington. While Washington teachers were satisfied with their conflict approaches and sustained strong ties and clear borders of their community, they tended to limit the nature of organizational changes in ways that reinforced existing community norms and values. In seeking unanimity, marginalizing dissent, transferring problems onto others, privatizing differences, and at times suppressing conflict, teachers diminished some opportunities for questioning and ultimately changing their beliefs and practices.

Individual Experiences

Because of Washington's tightly unified community and its close personal and professional ties, conflicts were viewed as extremely painful. Alternatively, when conflicts were quickly resolved or ended, these teachers felt a great sense of success and self-satisfaction with their ability to address conflicts. There was a connection between these two emotional states—fear of conflict with friends and happiness at success in handling conflicts in a way that sustained their ties. This in turn helped explain the low teacher turnover and high teacher satisfaction at Washington.

Conflicts were described as painful experiences for teachers that produced feelings of guilt, pain, and rejection. Alternatively, teachers also reported positive feelings about the school's ability to address conflict in a supportive way. If teachers' goals were to maintain their strong ties and sense of unity, then the manner in which they addressed conflicts was successful. They found themselves open to conflicts, able to talk them through and accommodate each other. Such strong unity and levels of trust expressed by teachers fostered a level of optimism about the outcome of conflicts.

Teachers reported a high level of satisfaction with how they handled conflicts. Sara, an eighth-grade teacher whose comments were typical of many others', characterized the faculty as able to resolve conflicts in ways that fostered unity. In contrast to her previous school, she noted:

I think this school is really good at talking about their problems. . . .
As far as the teachers go they will always hash out conflicts on an
issue. . . . I commend this school for that because in my other school
it didn't necessarily work out that way. I don't see our school as
ever being polarized like my old school.

Community Ties and Borders

As a result of the teachers' approach to conflict, their community was
highly unified (with small pockets of marginalized subgroups or individuals). Conflicts between teachers were quickly resolved, excluded, or
transferred and thus teachers maintained strong ties within the community. The bonds retained among Washington teachers were both personal
and professional. After a conflict, Washington teachers tended to emerge
more united than before. After the resolution of conflicts over the introduction of collaborative teaming reform, the teachers explained, "People
like each other here now." Similarly, a few days after a conflict within a
team, members let me know that they were "all smiles" now and had
worked out the problem swiftly.

Conflicts also further unified the Washington teacher community by
clearly defining outsiders beyond their borders. Solidarity was strengthened by their stance toward conflict, which often identified an outsider as
the problem or deferred conflict management to others such as the principal. Clear borders delineated those who could share in the benefits of the
community and those who were excluded.

These borders were best exposed in the conflict about problem students. When a teacher asked, "Are we really willing to suspend and expel
[problem students]?" another replied, "Aren't we going to support our
own?" thereby delineating insider and outsider status. Individuals who
were different or disagreed with the group were labeled resisters. They
were isolated, expelled, or absorbed. In a striking example, students were
referred to as "nons," meaning nonparticipants in the community. Exclusion of the nons or problem parents or resistant teachers all served to
reaffirm their own teacher community membership and bonds in opposition to the "others."

Organizational Change

Although conflicts within the community fostered some schoolwide
changes, such as reorganizing membership on teams or constructing
stronger discipline policies, the types of changes that occurred tended to
reinforce core norms, values, and practices already in existence within

the community. At times this meant that teaching and schooling beliefs and practices remained unchallenged and thus limited some important opportunities for change.

Conflicts over collaboration defined as "interpersonal" resulted in switching the players rather than fundamentally questioning norms of collaboration by opening up differences between colleagues. Dan, the science teacher on the eighth-grade team, may have had legitimate challenges to teaming based on disciplinary interests, conceptions of autonomy, professionalism, accountability, and meeting the needs of students. These substantive issues were left unexplored when the problem became identified as a personality deficit.

In conflicts about student concerns, teachers tended to maintain the status quo rather than examine different beliefs and practices around not reaching 30% of their student population. While teachers strengthened their discipline practices and their solidarity, they left unexplored teachers' expectations for students and values about changing core practices. They did not publicly disclose the gap between their stated goal that all students can learn and their daily talk and practices, which challenged this goal. They accepted, to some degree, that they would not reach the 30%.

Rather than explore this discrepancy as a means to challenge and change their teaching practices, they transferred the conflict elsewhere. During the time of my study, Washington teachers rarely inquired about, framed, or explored aspects of conflicts that would have questioned their shared norms and practices, nor did they seek solutions that dramatically challenged them.

CONCLUSION

Washington's is a community dedicated to a common vision of collaboration, interdependent work, consensus, and reform. It is ultimately a community of friends. They demonstrate an extraordinary capacity for collaborating on interdisciplinary grade-level teams and as a schoolwide professional community. They coordinate curriculum and reform efforts and share a common purpose in improving student achievement. At times they demonstrate the power of strong personal and professional ties. They speak the same language and can provide a united front for teaching and learning at Washington.

While demonstrating harmony and an uncanny ability to reach schoolwide consensus, the teacher community still experienced conflicts. Conflicts arose from their collaboration, both from introducing a community-building reform 10 years ago and from their ongoing teaming work. The eighth-grade Champions team's conflict with Dan demonstrated how teachers still struggled over community. Dan's objections to teaming, though, were labeled "resistance" by the rest of the team. The principal, an external authority, was asked to intervene to enforce his collaboration. Ultimately, Dan's objections were dismissed as a "personality deficit," rather than viewed as substantive dissent or a legitimate challenge about teacher autonomy within community. He continued to be perceived as an outsider to the teacher community, ultimately serving to define the borders of acceptable beliefs.

Teachers also engaged in conflicts about student concerns. There was a conflict between the school's vision statement about teacher expectations that "all students can learn" and teachers' public discourse about "problem students" that remained unexplored. By transferring the conflict onto students, teachers maintained a sense of solidarity and unity in opposition to "others." Thus Lani, representing problem students, would be suspended and isolated (quarantined from spreading a disease) from the community at large.

Meanwhile, teachers left unexamined a deeper conflict about how to meet the needs of up to 30% of their student population. When teachers began to raise some questions about changing practices, other teachers "circled the wagons," blaming students or parents, thus diminishing the responsibility for change within schools and the teacher community.

Ultimately, the teacher community tended to approach conflicts in ways that sustained their unity and organizational stability by arriving at rapid public consensus, excluding dissent, and privatizing conflicts or transferring them outside of their boundaries. This pattern resulted in very satisfied teachers who maintained their ties. This avoidant stance, though, limited the educational discussions and organizational changes that might have been necessary to address the needs of all their students.

NOTES

1. All participants were given pseudonyms to maintain confidentiality. Direct quotations were taken verbatim from participants.

2. All quantitative references in this chapter represent mean Likert scale values drawn from my teacher survey (Achinstein, 1997). Unless otherwise noted, the scale ranged from 1 to 5 where 1 represents "Strongly Disagree" and 5 represents "Strongly Agree." The "n" for Washington was 28 or 97% of certified staff. To see the specific survey items that made up the factor "Teacher learning community," and other concepts identified from the factor analysis, such as "Embracing conflict," "Avoiding conflict," and "Teacher stress," refer to Methodological Appendix.

3. I am relying here on retrospective interviews, which raises significant methodological questions. As teachers recall the conflict of 10 years ago, they have already begun to frame and make sense of the events given the subsequent history. However, teachers' construction (or reconstruction) of events does expose their current norms and beliefs about conflicts and helps reinforce my study of their current experiences with conflict.

4. All of these survey items are on a five-point Likert scale. While they demonstrate tendencies toward agreement or disagreement, most fell in the 3 range. Thus these are marginal distinctions. But I felt it important to address these surprising quantitative results.

CHAPTER 3

Chavez Middle School

It was August, a week before the students returned. The 42-member staff at Cesar Chavez Middle School gathered around a brightly covered table with candles and festive flowers in the faculty room. Shawna[1] began the day, setting the tone for the week of professional development. She was the director of Project Respect, a school reform and youth development program housed at Chavez addressing diversity and racism.

> This is work regarding race and culture. . . . We acknowledge that many are already working on this. But today is about us working as a community, doing it together. This work is for us to be a community where we are comfortable with our diverse staff. The purpose is that we want staff of color to stay and feel that they have a voice here. There is a tension in the work we will do. We want to make it comfortable for all, but some of the things we have to deal with are uncomfortable.

Embracing discomfort and exposing difficult conflicts were promoted as norms among Chavez teachers.

After watching a video, *The Color of Fear* (Wah, 1994), in which two African-Americans, two Latinos, two Asian-Americans, and one White man confront a racist White man, the whole faculty gathered to discuss their impressions and their own experiences with racism. Tami, an African-American teacher's aide, explained about her own schooling. "When my mother told me about the kings and queens of Africa and I told the nuns at Catholic school, they made me stand in the corner for I don't know how long. I was punished for trying to hear about my history." Lourdes, the drama teacher asked, "What is it to be an American? As a Latina, I struggle with that. I mean sometimes I feel as American as Apple pie." Max, an intern involved with school reform at Chavez through a support provider organization called Partners in School Innovation, added:

> I feel I have to speak, as the only Asian-American in the room. Often Asians are called invisible and we are often left out of the discus-

sions of race. . . . And when we talk about racism it's always Black and White. Where are the Asians? Conflicts between Asians and Blacks are called inter-ethnic conflict; they don't have the same status as racism.

Then Paul, a white guidance counselor for the eighth grade, contributed, "There were times I identified with the racist man in the video because I grew up in a racist household. . . . But I struggle with my guilt with this past." Miguel, a new Latino eighth-grade language arts/social studies teacher, encouraged him and said, "The first step is to acknowledge it. You can talk to me any time." Rachel, a White eighth-grade math/science teacher, recognized the "internalized racism" with which she grew up and explained that "none of my intimates are people of color. I am a racist. . . . My students call me racist." Beth, a White sixth-grade language arts/social studies teacher new to the school, leaned over to Rachel to say "that was very brave" to share.

At their next professional development meeting, the faculty formed caucuses by race to continue discussions. The groups split up between "people of color" and "White" teachers. The facilitators acknowledged that this was not ideal, as there were many different ethnicities and races represented here that had unique experiences. Interestingly, an African-American teacher chose to join the "White" teacher group. Inside the caucus session, Kati, a White eighth-grade teacher, criticized her school:

> I think a lot of us are comfortable here because it's quite elitist in its group membership. As far as group members, educationally it's exclusive. You need to know the [reform] language. There are contradictions here. . . . It's safe for me here. I'm White. But this institution is setting up White teachers to be saviors of kids of color.

In response, Mona, a White sixth-grade math/science teacher, said:

> I feel that it's sometimes painful, knowing it's a pretty liberal White middle-class vision for this school. I don't let that stop me from doing this work. Pain is a reminder it's not the answer to the oppressive structure we live in. I have to spend more time listening and thinking about how I can be truly anti-racist and make multicultural work that can really be transformational.

The principal, Julie, a White woman, concluded, "We need to be confident of who we are and that issues of race are out there. Our students need to see that we are keeping that in the forefront. . . . Kids know about racism. They are just seeing if we will wash over it. So first we must acknowledge it and then find ways to fight it and show them we are fighting it."

On the second day of the school year, despite many new faces in the room, these teachers were able to name and disclose the problem of racism in their midst, and take responsibility for it as adults. As I left that day, I was struck by a poster on the wall by the front entrance. A list of beliefs began, "All children should learn to live and work in a world that is characterized by interdependence and cultural diversity." These were the words one saw every day when entering and leaving Chavez Middle School. The entire staff's signatures appeared beneath the list of philosophical tenets.

THE SCHOOL

Chavez is an urban public school of 525 sixth- through eighth-grade students located in California. The white three-story building is a striking presence atop a hill, next to a fenced-in blacktop playground. The student body is diverse: 44% Latino, 29% African-American, 12.8% Other White, 7% Other Non-White, 3.4% Filipino, 2.9% Chinese, and .8% American Indian. Over one-quarter of the students are limited- or non-English speaking. Two-thirds are educationally disadvantaged youth, and 18% special education. Students come from low-income and racial-minority communities in the city and are bused into a primarily White middle-class neighborhood (Chavez Middle School Accountability Report Card).

The district in which Chavez is situated has experienced the turmoil of other diverse urban areas, including desegregation battles, budget crises, political controversies, and problems of a large bureaucracy. In 1979, the NAACP sued the district, charging that African-American students received a low-quality education. The suit was settled in 1982, when the district and the NAACP signed a "consent-decree," which set terms for school reform. U.S. appeals judge William Orrick approved the decree. The court decree impacted enrollment, curricula, and school programs. All schools must have at least four different racial groups, but not more than 45% of any one group. The decree also addressed expectations for students, parents, and teachers based on the 11 philosophical tenets (see Figure 3.1) that the faculty signed, thus demonstrating their commitment to meeting the needs of diverse students and fostering equity in education (Achinstein, Meyer, & Pesick, 1994; Kirp, 1982). As part of being hired at Chavez school, teachers agreed to uphold the tenets.

FIGURE 3.1. *Consent Decree Philosophical Tenets*

- All children should learn to live and work in a world that is characterized by interdependence and cultural diversity.

- All individuals are entitled to be treated with respect and dignity.

- All individuals want to learn and be recognized for their achievements.

- All individuals can learn.

- All individuals learn in many different ways and at varying rates.

- Each individual learns best in a particular way.

- All individuals are both potential learners and potential teachers.

- If individuals do not learn, then those assigned to be their teachers should accept responsibility for this failure and should take appropriate remedial action.

- Learning has both cognitive and affective dimensions.

- Learning can be subdivided into a number of specific, concrete competencies that can be used as a focus for teaching.

- Parents want their children to attain their fullest potential as learners and to succeed academically.

As a consent-decree school, Chavez had to meet certain standards each year and demonstrate improvement in specified areas, including student test scores. The district was under court pressure to meet consent-decree standards or close down three schools a year. In 1989 the district closed Chavez for not meeting the standards. Chavez students and teachers dispersed to five other schools. Then, in the middle of 1989, the school was reconstituted.

Reconstitution involved hiring a new staff, all of whom endorsed the consent-decree tenets. The school reopened with a new principal and an almost totally new faculty (only 10% of the former Chavez teachers remained). At that time the school experienced a shift in student population, from primarily African-American to predominantly Latino. In 1993, the district named Chavez a "CSIP" (Comprehensive School Improvement Program) school, designating it as "in trouble" and needing support to perform on 20 indicators or face reconstitution again. After improving read-ing and math achievement, the school was removed from the CSIP list without a second reconstitution. The school has documented improvements in student performance, a decline in disciplinary incidents, lower staff turn-over, and better school climate since 1992, when the faculty undertook numerous reforms.

Between 1989 and 1997, the school has had four principals. Julie, the principal during most of my study, was a White woman who had been at Chavez for 4 years. She left in 1997 and an African-American man became principal. Julie replaced a controversial figure who had created enough conflict with the staff that a district mediator came to the school to man-age these differences. Julie was seen as a team player, giving authority to teachers in shared decision-making. She was highly collaborative and de-fined her stance toward conflict as open, stating that "conversations about conflicts can create new ways of thinking and new ways of doing things."

Chavez is engaged in multiple regional and national reform initiatives. Chavez is a member of the Bay Area Coalition of Essential Schools (BAYCES). BAYCES is a regional affiliate of the national Coalition of Es-sential Schools (CES), which was established under the direction of Theodore Sizer of Brown University in 1984. There is no essential school "model;" rather, it is understood that each school must develop its own reforms based on its own setting and constituency, under the direction of common principles (Sizer, 1984). At the center of the principles lies a com-mitment to teach students to "learn to use their minds well." These habits call for students and teachers to actively voice opinions and critically re-flect on actions (Gerstein, 1995, p. 14). Other principles include that aca-demic and social goals of the school should apply to *all* students, and that a shift in authority relations in schools is needed to provide greater voice to teachers and students.

In 1991 Chavez received the 5-year State Board 1274 (SB 1274) grant that supported schools to voluntarily restructure themselves. SB 1274 fo-cuses on four main areas of improvement: instruction, curriculum, and assessment; redesigned school governance roles for parents and teachers; new options for students after 10th grade; and innovation in technology. The state initiative also supported school reform based on an inquiry pro-cess called "the protocol." In a protocol, colleagues share and critique their common work, from curriculum to schoolwide initiatives. They do so by examining data collected about their reform work. These inquiry and data-based procedures became an embedded part of professional work among faculty at Chavez.

They also applied for and eventually gained leadership status in the Bay Area School Reform Collaborative (BASRC). BASRC is a regional reform effort supporting school-based change efforts based on "focused efforts," as well as participation in a regionwide change initiative. BASRC encourages and funds schools to undertake a "cycle of inquiry," an action-research cycle whereby practitioners pose questions, collect and examine data, and determine actions for reform. Their focused effort of that reform was designed to promote the success of African-American and English Language Learner (ELL) students identified by the consent decree, who showed significantly less improvement than the general student population (BASRC application).

In all of these schoolwide efforts, Chavez faculty focused on teacher teaming and interdependent work, consensus-based decision-making, collective inquiry and critical reflection, schoolwide standards, high expectations for all students, and a commitment to respecting cultural diversity.

To sustain their reform work, a number of support providers worked with the Chavez faculty and community. Project Respect is a school reform and youth development program to promote equitable education for low-income students and students of color begun at Chavez Middle School. Project Respect staff were housed at Chavez and organized multiple opportunities for both adults and students. Their activities spanned formal and informal settings for reflection and action. They guided full-staff discussions on issues of race, culture, and sexual orientation. They also collaborated with students and parents to engage in consultations with faculty.

Project Respect activities held in more informal settings included "praxis groups," which involved reflective discussions among teachers engaging members in collective activities and inquiry about personal beliefs and practices. The term *praxis* refers to the reciprocal relationship between theory and practice, between reflection and action. Chavez teachers drew on this critical-theory term to shape the kinds of environments that encouraged reflection on their actions in order to transform their practices. These were unique settings for many faculty members, creating a space for personal reflection and exploration, as well as the conditions and expectations for fostering change. "Dialogue groups" between staff and students also offered an opportunity for teachers to listen to students.

Another organization involved in fostering reform work at Chavez was Partners in School Innovation, a nonprofit organization placing young interns in innovative schools to support their reform work for 2 years. The interns worked closely with administrators and teachers as reform coordinators, running meetings, facilitating conversations about reform, and supporting data collection and inquiry about reform outcomes. Each of Chavez's reform initiatives and support provider organizations also sought to build a strong teacher professional community at Chavez.

TEACHER COMMUNITY AT CHAVEZ

Chavez teachers were a diverse group, racially and in terms of their beliefs about teaching. The 42-member staff at Chavez is 61.9% Other White,
16.7% Latino, 14.3% African-American, 2.4% Other Non-White, 2.4% Filipino, and 2.4% Chinese (Chavez School Accountability Report Card). Hiring teachers of color to reflect their diverse student population was a concern of the school. The teachers were 64% female and 36% male. Many
teachers remarked on Chavez's high turnover rate as a source of instability in the school. Annual turnover was over 30% in the early 1990s and 17%
by 1996. There were reports of further decline in turnover to 10% in 1997.

Collaborative Practices

Chavez teachers collaborated on multiple levels: on grade-level interdisciplinary teams, called "families," which shared the same students; in
subject-matter departments that agreed to common performance standards;
and in schoolwide decision-making that engaged in whole-school reform.
They were extremely proficient with their carefully structured consensus
procedures for shared decision-making, which included opportunities to
raise new proposals, solicit dissenting opinions, engage in dialogue about
differences, and come to resolution.

By looking at the Chavez's teacher meeting schedule one immediately
sees the multiple opportunities and demands for collaboration (see Table
3.1). Formal collaboration included grade-level families, subject-matter
departments, curricular resource teams, the teachers' union, committees,
schoolwide faculty, the communitywide Restructuring Council (RC), and
more. The grade-level families met to plan curriculum and programs twice
a week. Departments discussed subject-matter standards and projects
weekly. Chavez had structured faculty meetings on Thursday mornings.
Students came to school late so the staff met as a whole group. The 20-
member Restructuring Council was the governing body for all school decisions and met two times a month. Seven teachers, five parents or community members, five students, two classified staff, and the principal
shared budget and curricular decision-making power.

What is less clear from this schedule is the informal collaboration at
Chavez. Teachers and students met in ongoing dialogue groups to discuss
issues of diversity. Teachers of color had organized lunches together a
couple of times. Nine teachers and staff members formed a praxis group
to discuss personal and professional concerns in a more personalized environment twice a month. Other teachers came together informally on
"T.G.I.F." occasions.

TABLE 3.1. *Chavez Teacher Meeting Schedule, 1996–1997*

PERIOD	MONDAY	TUESDAY	WEDNESDAY	THURSDAY	FRIDAY
AM	Administrators		Principal and Parent Teacher Association	Full Staff or Department or Family	
1			Counseling team 8th – LA/SS 8th – Math/Science		8th-grade Family
2		8th-grade Family	Counseling team 8th – LA/SS 8th – Math/Science		
3	6th – LA/SS	Restructuring Council and staff meeting Planning Team	6th – LA/SS 6th – Math/Science	6th-grade Family	
4			6th – LA/SS mtg. 6th – Math/Science	6th-grade Family	
Lunch	Union Building Committee	Special Education	Bilingual Immersion	IRISE meeting	
6		7th – LA/SS mtg.		7th – Math/Science	
7	7th-grade Family	7th – LA/SS mtg.	7th-grade Family Resource team	7th – Math/Science	
8		P. E. Dept. mtg.	Arts Dept.		
PM	Facilities Committee	Restructuring Council (bimonthly)	Healthy School Team	Hiring Committee	Student/Staff Dialogue Group

All meetings weekly, unless otherwise noted (Document, Nov. 4, 1996).

According to survey data, on items where they could strongly disagree (value of 1) to strongly agree (value of 5) with statements, teachers at Chavez reported a greater sense of cooperative effort among themselves (3.42) than isolation (2.76).[2] They agreed that they were continually learning and seeking new ideas from each other (3.58). The principal, Julie, described staff relations as a "community of learners."

> There's a lot of collaboration. . . . There are defined times set aside for grade-level collaboration and planning together, as well as subject area planning, and there are specific times set aside for schoolwide conversations and decision-making. Collaboration is very much in place as part of the culture of the school. The school in general is focused on a community of learners.

Even with all of this schoolwide collaboration, teachers identified as individuals, and with strong subgroups within their community. Ben, a teacher/reform coordinator at Chavez, explained that such individuality was a critical part of their collaboration.

> I think that's one of the key aspects of collaboration, that collaboration isn't about doing it one person's way. It's about maximizing the capacity of individuals to work together and to share. That should also include a nurturing of and recognition of their individual creativity and expression. . . . I think there's plenty of space for individual styles and priorities . . . and space for dissent here.

On a survey, teachers claimed a stronger identification as an individual or with a subgroup (grade-level team, subject department, teaching partner or peer, or racial group) (3.60) than as a whole-school community (2.79).

While the mandated collaborations at the school were supposed to foster ties between certain teachers, other teachers formed their own voluntary unofficial connections with like-minded peers. Kati, an eighth-grade teacher, distinguished between what she defined as her mandated artificial "professional" community and her voluntary peer community at the school. The professional community "is more your group because you are labeled a social studies teacher or an eighth-grade teacher." But when she described her unofficial peer community at the school, Kati said, "We can have a mutual sharing and discussion on ideas that goes two ways. . . . It's more of a meeting of capable minds that are willing to exchange and ask hard questions and work."

Teachers characterized a diversity of views and group identifications coexisting within the school, which were continuously debated. On a survey they tended to agree that "groups of teachers were very different from one another in terms of educational beliefs and practice" (3.53). Many teachers characterized multiple "camps." One camp was labeled by different teachers in the following ways: "liberal," "progressive," "low expectations," "racist," "the principal's camp," "relativistic," "subjective," "White middle-class," "affective," and "student-centered." Another was characterized as "authoritarian," "authoritative," "high expectations for students," "professional," "race conscious," "teacher-centered," "legalistic," "high accountability," "objective," "absolutist," and "judgmental."

The boundaries of membership of camps were fluid though, making them more like temporary allegiances based on a particular issue. Ben, a teacher/reform coordinator, explained that "it's not that there are camps; that sounds polarized. It's more of a spectrum of responses on specific issues." For example, over a conflict about preparing students for standardized testing, one teacher was "progressive" in being against "teaching to a test," and yet more "authoritarian" when it came to issues of discipline.

Nor did race consistently divide teachers. A number of White teachers aligned themselves with the "higher expectations and stronger discipline" group at the school, as opposed to teachers who may have a more "relativistic" or "liberal attitude." In a vivid demonstration of the fluidity of social allegiances, when the staff was asked to divide up into caucuses by race to discuss issues of diversity at the school, an African-American teacher chose to join the group of White teachers. Other teachers crossed camp lines identifying themselves as "student-centered" and yet upholding "high accountability" for both teachers and students.

Nonetheless, some racial differences among staff perceptions were identified. On a survey, teachers of color at Chavez reported stronger agreement (4.08) with the statement "groups of teachers are very different" than did White teachers (3.28). White teachers also said they felt a greater sense of being a "teacher learning community" (3.27) than did teachers of color (2.83). Teachers of color tended to agree that racial and ethnic differences among staff members divided the staff (3.36) more so than White teachers (2.33). Such responses reflect a pattern in the larger society that Whites and people of color experience race quite differently.

Ideological Stance

Although Chavez faculty agreed that groups of teachers were very different from one another in their educational beliefs and practice, the teacher community did hold common educational visions as reflected in their mission statement, work with students, and conversations. Such a shared conception about the role of schooling in society served to unite a differentiated staff.

This educational ideology was tied to Chavez's consent decree and desegregated status. Behind the consent-decree and desegregation goals lay a conception of school as a site for societal transformation, and the teachers that applied and came to the school embraced such values. Samuel, an African-American eighth-grade language arts/social studies teacher reflecting the critical ideology of the faculty, explained that he saw education as "changing the society, changing attitudes, changing issues of power, making social change. . . . I see what education should be as liberatory; it's to challenge the existing social system, to change it."

There was a focus on social justice in schooling seen in the teachers' commitment to innovative pedagogy and relevant curriculum for their student population. Teachers engaged students in discussion-based and student-centered learning. The Chavez teacher community's educational ideology was in line with critical theorists such as Giroux, who see the purpose of schooling as social transformation (1988). "Public schools," Giroux writes, "need to be organized around a vision that celebrates not what is but what could be, a vision that looks beyond the immediate to the future, and a vision that links struggle to a new set of human possibilities" (p. 10). As Ben explained, "I think that we have, here, a lot of people who come from political activist backgrounds in some way, shape, or form so their critical thinking skills and capacities are pretty well developed." Such values about education often placed critique, struggle, resistance, and conflict at the center of teachers' work.

Such a critical ideology was carried out in Chavez's reform practices, as exemplified in their reform work with BASRC. Teachers publicly identified disproportionate student achievement by race and class as a problem of inequity. Their values were heard in the language of the following report developed by the staff:

> While we have explored the issue somewhat, our school staff has not adequately developed the repertoire of instructional and interpersonal skills and strategies necessary to promote success for diverse student populations, in particular low-income African-Americans and English language learners. The dominant teaching practices still favor middle-class students who have internalized many of the passive learning habits necessary for success in the culture of traditional schooling. Our classroom GPA data, disaggregated by ethnicity, supports this conclusion. (BASRC Funding Application)

In this statement, teachers critically reflect on their own responsibility and institutional culpability in perpetuating classism and racism. Further, the staff identified a concern about enforcing assimilation at the cost of losing a student's cultural identity. The report goes on to state, "Students who are not a part of this dominant culture experience marginalization, and can equate doing well in school with 'selling out' their own cultural identity" (BASRC Funding Application).

CONFLICTS AT CHAVEZ

When conflict is brought to the surface, people are uncomfortable with it. That's when it becomes real.

—Samuel, Eighth-grade teacher

I thought it was real [when we had conflict]. It was going somewhere. People had to grapple with something that's discomforting. That is important to the process of getting better as far as defining a schoolwide response.

—Kati, Eighth-grade teacher

It may be uncomfortable when we have conflicts. But we may need conflicts to resolve things. We can't just have the status quo.

—Shawna, Project Respect Director

Chavez teachers engaged in multiple conflicts. The responses to each conflict encountered were remarkably similar—the teachers publicly exposed, explored, and at times embraced conflicts, reflecting on their practices and beliefs in efforts to fundamentally change their school. As the three Chavez staff comments above disclose, "when conflict is brought to the surface" that's "when it becomes real." "It was going somewhere," which is "important to the process of getting better" or changing "the status quo." Embracing conflict offered a promise of change and thus was considered a positive professional habit at Chavez.

Overview of Conflicts

Conflict between teachers was abundant and publicly vocalized at Chavez. Conflicts about teacher collaboration and those about student concerns encompass two broad categories of teacher disputes at the school. Conflicts over teacher collaboration involved schoolwide controversies about: hiring more teachers of color; curriculum, pedagogy, and standards of practice; and addressing the achievement gap between students of color and White students. Inter-team conflicts included teams' roles in contributing to and responsibility for upholding schoolwide agreements. Intra-team conflicts involved confrontations about individual accountability to team policies. Conflicts about student concerns included disagreements over discipline beliefs and policies, disputes about how best to reach African-American students, and concerns about addressing the needs of special education students.

There was a recognizable pattern of responses to these conflicts. Teachers tended to solicit differences in belief and practice, explore these conflicts publicly and collectively, and thus foster opportunities for change within teachers and across the school. As they engaged in inquiry processes that explored the complexities that lay behind many of their conflicts, they tended to experiment with different kinds of solutions, continually negotiating and renegotiating in response to dilemmas that were not easily solved. (See Figure 3.2 for a summary of conflict types, approaches, and outcomes at Chavez.)

By examining in greater detail some specific instances of conflict about collaboration and about student concerns, we can see the recurring themes of embracing conflict at Chavez. The next section explores each type of conflict, specifically highlighting one major vignette under each category that details this recurring stance. The particular vignettes were chosen because they were representative of the conflict responses exhibited in most other conflicts at Chavez during the course of my study, and expose dominant patterns in relation to managing conflict within the teacher professional community.

Conflicts About Collaboration

Collaboration was particularly conflict-ridden at Chavez as teachers openly identified their divergent beliefs and group identifications. The ethnic and racial diversity of Chavez's staff impacted conflicts about collaboration as well. Finally, encouraging subgroup affiliation through grade-level families and subject-matter departments may have further exacerbated collaboration conflicts.

At the forefront of all of Chavez's collaboration conflicts was a concern about "accountability" to one's colleagues and to the students. By accountability, teachers meant responsibility for upholding collectively agreed on norms and practices. Ultimately, accountability to one's colleagues was connected to accountability to the students. Conflicts arose when teachers were perceived as not actively participating in or, in some cases, undermining collaboration by going against shared decisions.

A report reflecting on 5 years of reform at the school documented that teachers wanted "clearer accountability about the level and nature of collaboration required. This applie[d] not just to teacher curricular collaboration, but to larger forms of collaboration within grade level, subject area,

FIGURE 3.2. *Conflict Types, Approaches, and Outcomes at Chavez*

TYPE OF CONFLICT	APPROACHES	OUTCOMES
Conflicts about Collaboration:		
Schoolwide		
Conflict over racial diversity of staff and need to hire more teachers of color. Faculty debate meaning of affirmative action.	Faculty meetings discuss hiring. Hiring committee forms and debates meaning of affirmative action. Project Respect facilitates professional development on racism and diversity.	Hired more teachers of color. Initiated teachers of color lunches. Ongoing work with Project Respect.
Curriculum and pedagogical conflicts about schoolwide curricular standards. Conflicts over best approach to multicultural curriculum and pedagogy. Conflicts over methods and priority of preparing students for standardized testing. Identify testing gap between students of color and Whites.	Public discussion and debate at grade-level teams and in full faculty meetings. Examination of curricular/pedagogical issues through inquiry around different practices and student test scores.	Ongoing discussion and experimentation. Move toward some shared standards, and flexibility of practice within. Introduce new ways to better prepare students for testing and to address gap between students of color and white students. Ongoing professional development about equitable teaching practices.
Inter-team		
Conflict with "marginalized" (art) departments feeling left out of the decision-making loop.	Faculty meeting to discuss. One art teacher raises continued concerns about having a voice in decision-making.	Hire more art teachers. Form a department with meeting times. Still some isolation of arts team.
Intra-team		
Conflict about individual teacher's obligations and accountability to teaming when certain teachers would not participate in team activities.	Team confronts individual to set norms. Team meets with administrator. Team begins "process meetings."	End "process meetings." Switch facilitators. Teacher still minimally participates.

FIGURE 3.2. *Cont.*

TYPE OF CONFLICT	APPROACHES	OUTCOMES
Conflicts about Students:		
Discipline		
Conflicts over discipline policies and attitudes. Teachers state that they are sending too many African-American students to the office for discipline. Differences in schoolwide and grade-level discipline procedures. Teachers feel others are not upholding responsibility for discipline.	Faculty discussion of sending too many African-American students to office. Discussion in faculty meetings and grade levels about consistency in disciplinary procedures. Eighth grade made disciplinary proposal to faculty. Grade-level meeting with administrators.	New proposal of discipline plan presented by eighth-grade team to school. After input from faculty, new administrative team sets goals and expectations for discipline and presents them to full faculty—an appreciative audience.
Reaching Certain Student Populations		
Conflicts over reaching African-American students result in debate over piloting IRISE program.	IRISE debates in faculty and Restructuring Council meetings on integration and desegregation goals of school. Public debates over issue of tracking by race. Disagreement about teachers' level of expectations for students of color discussed in team and faculty meetings. Project Respect activities with teachers and students about diversity.	Pilot IRISE and discuss expansion of program. Hold a Racial Harmony Conference. Continue to expand role of Project Respect in professional development and activities on diversity. A teacher published the writings of his Asian student who expressed feelings of marginalization because of her race—resulted in classroom discussions throughout the school and developed Asian Students lunches.
Special education inclusion: Debates over best way to include special education students. Difficulty with mainstreaming without resource teacher's support.	Grade-level discussions on inclusion. Teaming experiment by 2 special ed. teachers with regular ed. teachers. Concern by some teachers who don't know how to meet special education students' needs. Teacher talks to special education teacher.	Ongoing experiments with inclusion of special education in mainstreamed classes.

or with the counseling department" (SB 1274 Summary Analysis, p. 22). Tanya, an eighth-grade math/science teacher, whose concerns reflected those of many others, explained:

> Accountability is the big issue. There is none. [Laughs.] I don't think there is accountability on the part of teachers being accountable for themselves, what we're doing in our classroom, are we servicing our students? Or accountable [to other teachers]. Are we doing what we agree to do? Because we all agreed to do that and yet people don't. Are we agreeing to follow the agreements?

Schoolwide Collaboration Conflicts. Teachers at Chavez thought that ac-countability to students meant having a staff that more accurately reflected the racial makeup of the student body. As a faculty they debated how to diversify their staff, what hiring practices that promoted affirmative ac-tion should look like, and how to retain teachers of color. As the hiring committee began discussing candidates, a conflict arose about the mean-ing of affirmative action.

Tanya, an African-American eighth-grade math/science teacher, de-scribed a conflict that arose during the hiring procedures. She identified how she and Jake, a White music teacher, debated the meaning of affirma-tive action.

> Jake was saying, "Well we need to hire this person [of color]. We don't have a choice. We have to look at affirmative action." I'm like, "that is not it. . . . If that's what our affirmative action policy is then we all need to agree to that. I'm not going to agree to that. We need to take it to the staff to discuss this is what we decided and why." Then I got real plain, and said what I thought affirmative action was.
>
> My understanding of [affirmative action] is you do not neces-sarily hire a person of color or a woman because of who they are. It's more about making the process open to groups of people who would not necessarily have the opportunity available to them and giving them an equal chance of getting that position. . . . If we did hire a person of color and we felt they weren't qualified, we'd have to decide, did we feel that what we saw was worth hiring and make sure we could support them so that they did become qualified, as opposed to just hiring them because of who they are.

While both teachers agreed on the fundamental premise that they should hire more people of color, they differed on how to choose candidates and how to support them, once at the school. Other teachers, citing the problem of teachers of color leaving the school, identified the need for ongoing support.

Tanya explained how the opportunity to debate these meanings and hear other teachers' concerns allowed for changes in Jake's understandings and ultimately in the hiring of more teachers of color who would receive the support they needed to be fully qualified. She said, "Jake came more toward my way of thinking I believe in the end. I think because there was a discussion and I think he also heard other people voicing their concerns." Furthermore, "teachers-of-color lunches" were initiated as a result of teachers' sharing their sense of a lack of support at Chavez.

Teachers also debated how to address the achievement gap between students of color and White students. The principal brought achievement data to a staff meeting and pointed out the gap between students of color and Whites. After examining data collected about student achievement, teachers engaged in curricular and pedagogical discussions about how to prepare students for standardized tests, how to reach different kinds of learners, and how teachers' expectations impact student achievement. Throughout all of these discussions, teachers voiced different philosophies about ways to meet the needs of their diverse students, while collectively remaining committed to doing so. Some teachers denigrated a "teach to the test" approach, while others warned that these tests were important gatekeepers that often excluded children of color from educational attainment. They also debated the kinds of schoolwide curricular standards to support. The entire staff worked with Project Respect and other support providers to explore different pedagogical and curricular approaches to meet their students' needs. Ultimately, teachers agreed to schoolwide standards and some practices about test preparation, while continuing to debate implementation at the grade level and individual level.

Inter- and Intra-team Conflicts. Conflicts also arose between teams. At a full faculty meeting, the art department teachers publicly confronted other teams about feeling marginalized from grade-level-based and schoolwide decision-making. They felt overburdened by working with every student in the school and isolated without opportunities to meet as a team (because of grade-level–family team meetings). The resolution was to hire another art teacher and to create a time for the art department to meet as a team.

Accountability to collaborate created intra-team conflicts as individual teachers did not participate in grade-level activities or hold up their end of teaming. These issues arose at team-level meetings as teachers sought to hold each other accountable to teaming.

The Eighth-grade "Family" Conflict. While no two teams at Chavez were exactly alike (the eighth grade was often described as more "conflictual" than other teams), the eighth-grade conflicts that arose and their subsequent responses were in many ways typical of the larger community's experience. This vignette illustrates how members of the Chavez teacher professional community acknowledged and critically reflected on differences and conflicts among colleagues. While these teachers remained frustrated and found no final resolution to their team conflict, they explored some of the complexities of negotiating a role for individualism within community. They were able to name this intractable dilemma of community that lay beneath the conflict.

The eighth-grade family argued about teaming, particularly about how to handle their individual differences. The 12 members of this family included four math/science teachers (one of whom was a retired business executive who taught part time), three language arts/social studies teachers (one of whom taught bilingual immersion and another who taught in the African-centered program), a special education teacher, a resource teacher, a counselor, an art teacher, and an intern from Partners in School Innovation. The group included six women and six men. The racial breakdown was four people of color (two African-Americans, one Latino, and one Asian-American) and eight Whites. Periodically, Dora, an assistant principal (a Latina female), joined the family meetings as well.

The eighth-grade-level family met twice a week for 50 minutes during the school day to address common policies (discipline, grading, fieldtrip procedures); curriculum (culminating performance exhibitions of student research, portfolios); common programs (graduation, assemblies, parent-night); shared student concerns (student study teams to discuss progress of individuals); and schoolwide decision-making (reports to and from the Restructuring Council, reactions to schoolwide proposals).

The team had a history of conflict about issues of accountability for collaboration. In 1994–1995, the team struggled, with one member not coming to group meetings and others not fulfilling their agreed-on responsibilities. Team members identified themselves as strong on "individuality," and reported that collective action was sometimes a challenge. In the spring of 1995, members of the team reflected on what was not working and documented a lack of time and organization, and a need to improve "commitment to the family and respect for each other" (Eighth-grade family document).

In the fall of 1995, the whole team spent long hours reflecting on shortcomings in their process and developing group norms to hold each other accountable, to open avenues of communication, and to air differences. After much discussion, the group developed new norms that, among other items, included the following:

- Members will disagree agreeably.
- A process observer will report on group process at the end of each meeting.
- Family members will show sensitivity toward different cultures and personal styles.
- Members will be flexible about differences. (Eighth-grade family document)

Nonetheless, throughout my observations of the team in 1996–1997, teachers demonstrated low levels of participation in family activities, including struggling to find volunteers to be the facilitator or notetaker at meetings and grade-level representative at the Restructuring Council meetings.

In the fall of 1996, as the team met to renew their group norms, Samuel, an African-American language arts/social studies teacher who had been the family facilitator in 1995 and actively involved in generating the 1995 norms refused to endorse them. He felt that teachers had not been held accountable to them previously, nor would be again. Samuel also opted out of participating in a grade-level disciplinary policy (involving a lunch-time detention) because he felt that teachers were not carrying their own disciplinary responsibility in their classrooms.

The team members confronted Samuel, who would not agree to the norms, and asked the group members from the previous year to meet together, along with administrators, to resolve the issue. Kati, a White language arts/social studies teacher, went to each of the eighth-grade teachers to solicit an agenda for the meeting. As the family began to mobilize to discuss collaborative agreements, Carla, a White special education teacher, described to me an eighth-grade history of confronting conflicts.

> We're used to getting down and talking about issues. We had a real vested interest in maintaining being able to work together as a family. Because we started out the year and put a lot of time to try to lay the groundwork to get the family working together. . . . We worked on basic skeleton suggestions for what the norms would be and what we expect of people, and analyzing what didn't work in the past so that we could go forward. Then we brought that to the planning meetings. The whole family really felt solid about the way we were starting up the year. And like I said it all kind of fell apart. I think that's where our history of being able to talk to each other about this stuff came from. And also it was agreed upon that we would talk about stuff in the family meetings if it came up, that somebody wasn't doing their job.

At the meeting, Kati opened the discussion with concerns about professionalism and participation. She identified the need for "administrative support after inter-family problem-solving failed on issues of professionalism, interaction, participation in family meetings, and members of family sabotaging the team." The principal, Julie, responded that the teachers needed to come to common agreements and hold each other responsible, saying, "You need to establish a relation so that you can approach that person and say, 'I, no, *We* need your support.'" Samuel remarked that this "was tried last year and did not work."

In the course of the meeting, teachers identified the conflict as "not just a personality problem." Samuel saw it as a clash of communication styles:

> In terms of norms, we laid out how to talk to each other using "I statements" and not raising our voices. . . . I found those ridiculous constraints, maybe partly a gender and cultural thing. I believe that dealing with a conflict straight on directly is not disrespectful. Those norms meant putting you in a box of how to act.

Teachers also framed the conflict as an organizational problem. Rachel, a White math/science teacher, and Kati were concerned about both administrative accountability in enforcing teacher requirements and problems with the power and authority of "teachers policing teachers."

Some identified the conflict as rooted in a larger dilemma about how communities accommodate individual differences. Gary, the part-time math teacher, closed the meeting with the following comment about the delicate balancing act of fostering individualism within a group.

> I think what this group is struggling with is to what extent to accommodate individuals to do their own things without abusing the group. It's a gray issue. . . . I suggest you take some time and come back to this later and think about how to accommodate each other as individuals.

While some were pleased by an opportunity to air the problems, no resolution occurred. The eighth-grade team meetings ran pretty much the same as usual. The dissenting teacher, Samuel, still did not agree to participate in the group norms. Throughout conversations during the year with team members, most identified the team as "dysfunctional." Some spoke very rarely during meeting times. Miguel, a new Latino language arts/social studies teacher, felt he was being socialized into a bad dynamic and chose not to participate. "I just listen. I don't want to be part of it . . . because I don't think I'm learning anything positive or productive from this."

Other interventions were tried, including a month-long series of "process discussions" facilitated by two support providers at the school. Talking individually to teachers first about concerns with the team, the two facilitators, Shawna, a White director of Project Respect, and Max, an Asian-American intern with Partners in School Innovation, came to the group and began a process of reflections. Shawna introduced the work to the team in the following way:

> This process is going to be difficult at times. It may be uncomfortable when we have conflicts. But we may need conflicts to resolve things. We can't just have the status quo. . . . If you do feel uncomfortable, bring it up. Don't just stop there and withdraw. Hopefully, we can talk about tough issues, and issues that deal with the family, the whole school, and your work here. This process discussion will be ongoing. It's really important to make everyone feel comfortable, as comfortable as possibly can be expected in dealing with tough issues.

The group reflected, in writing and conversations, on what was working and not working for the team. The facilitators broke down the reflective comments into four categories, demonstrating the multidimensionality of the problems:

1. meeting topics (trivial)
2. meeting process (clearer role and responsibility definition)
3. interpersonal (sense of intimidation, silencing, belief that others aren't doing right by the kids)
4. larger context (too much to do, stress, accountability, turnover, not treated as professional) (Eighth-grade family document)

While these process discussions were slow, with little active participation, the group developed new norms and agreed to "be direct with each other" and "air differences." After all, as Rachel explained to the team, "the goal is not to be friends, but to work together."

There was, however, a rising sense of frustration with the process discussions. Tanya, an African-American math/science teacher, declared her frustration in a meeting as she explained that they were leaving "unresolved a deeper dilemma of accountability within the school." After 4 weeks of such meetings, the group decided to end the intervention and meet only once a week (they had been meeting once a week for business and another day on process). Carla explained, "When we are having a meeting to have a better meeting, I know we're having too many meetings."

Participants also described a painful recognition that the process discussions made public deeper value conflicts and debates, which they may not have wanted to unravel. Samuel likened the discomfort to pulling at a loose thread and realizing that to get at the issue meant unraveling the whole sweater. He explained, through an imaginary dialogue, why he thought the process discussions in the eighth-grade team would not succeed:

> People are just not interested, not really, because it's a bigger issue than that. It's like saying, "Oh, let's just pull this little, loose thread here."
> "Oh, no, that's all right. Leave it."
> "No, let me just get the little thread for you."
> "No, really, just leave it. It's all right."
> Then they pull it and all of a sudden, zip!! You've got a big old nothing [demonstrates pulling apart the sweater]
> "Sorry."
> "That's why I told you not to pull the little thread!"
> "But it's just a little thread. "
> "I know you saw it as a little thread and you're going to do everybody a favor. But I knew you were going to mess up my whole job, tear up my whole sleeve."

Other teachers' comments about eighth-grade team conflicts highlighted the perception that they needed to take greater ownership of the problem, that they were not really confronting the conflict. Some participants said that people should be even more confrontational in style. Kati said, "That would look like people screaming at each other. . . . It would mean people getting real, if that meant people having an argument—God forbid—then that's what it should look it. But I've seen people are just not bothering to get to that stage anymore."

Some teachers described a sense of frustration and despair about any changes regarding accountability. Kati pulled back from participating in other teacher collaborations because of her sense of disillusionment about accountability to teaming. Others were more optimistic about the eighth-grade teaming process as they looked over a longer period of time. Shawna explained her analysis of the nature of change and learning in the eighth-grade team.

> Some people, maybe not this time, but over time, are learning. [They are recognizing,] "Oh, this is why this is going on. Oh, we had a problem here. Oh, we need to do something about this." They are . . . [learning] very slowly and very unevenly.

The eighth-grade meetings hardly changed after the process discussions. Samuel, who had resisted the norms at the beginning of the year, continued to contribute minimally to the group. The group continued to try to engage him, while allowing him distance. The team also supported Samuel in initiating a new program for at-risk African-American students, allowing him to teach fewer students. Other teachers rarely volunteered for team activities.

One major change did occur mid-year, however, when the teacher facilitator of the meetings switched roles with another eighth-grade teacher. The team successfully planned graduation activities and performed the functions of a grade-level team. Two of the eighth-grade teachers, Kati and Tanya, changed their roles in the 1997–1998 school year (one worked part-time in the district and part-time at Chavez as a restructuring coordinator, another pursued graduate studies and worked at Chavez part-time). Two teachers from other grades joined the team as well. Common agreements had to be continually negotiated. In a strong tradition of raising conflict, some teachers were more optimistic than others about the team's ability to continue this negotiation process.

Conflicts About Student Concerns

As accountability to colleagues became a source of conflict for teachers, so too did their accountability to students. Conversations about approaches to teaching a diverse student population including concerns about curriculum and pedagogy, standards, discipline, assessment, special education inclusion, bilingual immersion, and racial integration became occasions for teacher controversy.

Teachers' Responsibility for "All Students." Because Chavez is a consent-decree school, teachers had an added responsibility to support *all* students' development. Chavez teachers described a strong degree of commitment to their students, identifying with student problems and expressing responsibility for addressing student failures. The words on the wall as one entered the school echoed this sentiment: "If individuals do not learn, then those assigned to be their teachers should accept responsibility for this failure and should take appropriate remedial action" (Consent Decree Tenets).

This commitment to addressing student concerns was heard as teachers formally gathered in a series of faculty meetings to review their school site plan. At one such faculty meeting, one group of teachers challenged the language of the document about "decreasing the number of low-performing students" (referred to as "lower quartile" on standardized testing). Alice, a library media teacher, reported that the text was written in a way that implied solutions of removing or excluding students, rather than teachers' taking responsibility for improving student performance. She explained the difficulty with the wording to the group:

> Does "decrease lower quartile students" mean to help them learn or get better students? I found that disturbing. It's not that we get different students and boot these ones out. Do we mean to eliminate lower-quartile students from the Chavez population, or exclude them, or single them out, which would not be inclusion? . . . Do we want to eliminate them or raise their status and skills?

The group agreed to clarify the language with the rest of the staff.

Chavez had many mechanisms for openly raising and addressing conflicts about students' race and culture. Throughout the year faculty publicly engaged in professional development, dialogue, and debate over student diversity (e.g., consent-decree week, professional development on heterosexism, reflections on diverse test scores of racial groups, debates on a multicultural conference, reflective "praxis" groups, and dialogue groups with students). Teachers acknowledged that they talked about these difficult issues. Catherine, a White seventh-grade language arts/social studies teacher, explained:

> We talk about race, class, culture, gender issues, and sexuality issues. We talk about those issues in an up-front fashion, but probably not enough. . . . When we have time together, it's on our agenda. . . . I think some of the systems we have in place have helped us with that. . . . When we do talk, what we do is we raise the issues. They're difficult issues.

The outcomes of these activities resulted in some organizational changes including hiring more teachers of color; introducing an African-centered pilot program; organizing student-teacher dialogue groups; initiating an Asian-American cultural group; and designing a new schoolwide standardized test-preparation procedure to address inadequate gains in African-American test scores.

While the staff was engaged in numerous activities around race and equity, Chavez teachers remained critical of their responses concerning student diversity. Many participants agreed that Chavez "should" but often did not address conflicts about race and culture deeply and meaningfully. Some found low levels of conflict resolution, while others criticized the school for moving to "quick fixes" rather than addressing deeper issues. Peter, a White sixth-grade math/science teacher, put it this way, "It's almost like we do this superficial embrace [of the conflict] but we don't really look at what the problem is."

The IRISE Debates. In faculty meetings in the 1995–1996 school year, the faculty began to address the issue of teacher accountability for low student achievement and the high rate of disciplinary referrals of African-American students. Teachers expressed concerns that "we are sending too many African-American boys to the counseling office" (Peter, a White sixth-grade math/science teacher), and, more generally, "we are not meeting the needs of our African-American youth whom we are supposed to address as a consent-decree school" (Gary, a White eighth-grade math teacher).[3]

In response, the faculty began a discussion about piloting a district-initiated experimental program called IRISE (Infusing Responsibility for Intellectual and Scholastic Excellence), which involved African-centered curriculum and pedagogy. Eve, an African-American assistant principal, was active in creating the program at the district level, and supported a pilot at Chavez. Two African-American teachers, Larry and Samuel, were trained over the summer and proposed trying the program in four classes of 15 African-American low-achieving students, who would spend half the day in an African-American-only setting. The program's goals included language acquisition, disseminating cultural precepts, and mathematics proficiency utilizing "African-centered" content.

In the spring of 1996, conflict arose at a faculty meeting where discussion about adopting the IRISE program was to take place. Due to some error, the pilot teachers were omitted from the agenda. Proponents of the program spoke up in anger about "their voices needing to be heard," "the issue being swept under the rug," and the success of African-American youth needing to be addressed. Gary explained the tone of the meeting:

> There was anger, passion, and very strong language. People were being very emotional in their choice of words. . . . People were insisting that they had not been heard in the past, that they weren't going to be ignored any more. . . . There were some people who were saying that this school, the faculty and administration had not taken responsibility for making African-American students succeed.

Finally, the pilot teachers spoke. In the discussion that followed, some teachers voiced support for the program in terms of meeting the needs of underserved African-American students who were targeted as part of Chavez's consent-decree mission. They also saw the program as addressing an equity issue, because Latino students already received benefits and resources beyond those of their African-American counterparts through a bilingual immersion program. Further, advocates hoped the program would help remedy the issue of faculty sending primarily African-American youth to the counseling office for discipline.

In response, other teachers, such as Peter, asked, "Is this segregation and retracking after desegregation?" In a school that had worked so hard to integrate its diverse populations and to build on racial and ethnic harmony, wasn't this a step away from its desegregation goals? Some teachers also expressed concern about how the small class sizes for IRISE would impact the rest of the faculty's teaching load.

In interviewing the staff about the decision to pilot IRISE, I heard multiple ways of framing the conflict and a recognition by all that there were varied beliefs about how best to reach African-American students at Chavez. In particular, Chavez teachers identified the conflict over IRISE as about resources and values in addressing diverse students.

Some teachers saw the conflict in organizational terms. For them, the conflict was over equitable funding for African-American students or fair allocation of class sizes. Some teachers, like Gary, argued that consent-decree money was not "really being targeted to benefit the African-American students, who, in theory, it is supposed to help." Some, like Peter, Samuel, and Carmen, a Latina sixth-grade Spanish-immersion teacher, spoke of school as a "money game" connected to "power" and "influence." Others identified the conflict as over resources for teachers, since smaller class sizes for IRISE teachers meant bigger classes for others. Anna, a White sixth-grade math/science teacher, concluded, "The whole demands of the staff . . . implementing IRISE were fairly unreasonable. For IRISE to have a class size of 15 when everybody else has class sizes of 30 assigned seems to be unfair."

What made the response to this conflict unusual at Chavez was that beyond a battle over resources, teachers opened up a public debate over institutional issues. They identified the normative and value debates about how to reach African-American students. Peter explained, "A larger conflict is what spawned the IRISE thing, is just the question of how we deal with African-American [students] who are failing at Chavez. . . . For years and years it seems we haven't done anything about it."

Teachers acknowledged that the IRISE conflicts were over basic values and goals about integration, tracking, segregation, and desegregation. As Tanya, an African-American eighth-grade math/science teacher expressed it, "We have not yet agreed on philosophy." Peter also explained the conflict in relation to clarifying conceptions of integration:

I think people recognize that it's an issue. It should be handled. It's an important issue. But in my opinion, it's never been articulated what the issue is. Or it's never been spelled out what is the goal, like what do we want. O.K., we want kids of different colors getting along. O.K., fine. Now, how are we going to do it? No one's ever done that process.

Chavez teachers disagreed on methods for integration. Some found segregation a means for greater long-term integration. Carmen explained:

If being in IRISE builds African-American students' self-esteem then when they are mixed, there will be less conflict. Why do we expect if we mix them that they would initially get along? First, we need to work on what's good about themselves.

A number of teachers, including Carmen, Kati, and Peter, mentioned that de facto "tracking" by race already occurred at Chavez because the Latino students predominated in some classrooms where the teachers were certified for second-language learners.

Tanya began to question her stance on segregation and integration because of Chavez's inability to reach some African-American students. She turned to IRISE as a way to address this lack.

Are we really segregating the kids? Well, yeah, we are. People see segregation as a totally negative thing. I don't necessarily see that's true. I definitely am an integrationist, but at the same time I don't feel like the structures in this school work for a certain population of the African-American community. I think that this program has a chance of doing that if it's done well.

In opposition, other teachers expressed concern about resegregating students after legal desegregation had occurred. Peter said, "That's tracking and that's segregating, and what are the implications of that?" Such opinions were shared publicly in faculty meetings. Kati said, "We worked so hard to integrate and have heterogeneous classes and now you want to go this way?"

Uncovering even deeper roots behind the IRISE conflict, some teachers (including both Whites and teachers of color) identified racism among their colleagues. Samuel said, "Bottom line is African-American students do not feel welcome at this school. . . . They don't feel that they have been getting what they need and what they deserve." Anna, a White sixth-grade math/science teacher, identified "White privilege" as a problem. "I think that the staff of color feels like the White staff has a tendency to be unaware of their privilege. . . . We are insensitive to the fact that people of color don't have as broad a choice as we do to be heard." Samuel went so far as to describe the problem of racism in education in the following way: "I see a lot of miseducation around here in the plantation we call Chavez Middle School." Carmen identified a connection between racism and teachers' not holding high enough standards for youth of color. Such teachers, she noted, "end up sending African-American students to the counseling office and expecting less of them."

The IRISE debates raised questions about conceptions of schooling and change. Teachers' discussion of how to create equity and support the achievement of all students extended beyond the school walls to the larger society. Samuel explained his support of the IRISE program as part of "liberatory" form of education that challenged the "existing society."

After much discussion in full faculty meetings, Restructuring Council meetings, and informal gatherings, the faculty reached consensus to try IRISE as an experiment. There was a recognition that the status quo was not working—that, as Anna put it, "we need to try something different with this group of kids." They agreed to pilot the project in two classrooms and evaluate its impact throughout the year. Peter explained, "I think there was some trepidation but I also think . . . that people said, 'O.K. let's try it. . . . Yeah, but let's see if it works. Let's try anything. What's been going on certainly isn't working.'"

In the winter of the first year of IRISE implementation, Chavez teachers discussed plans for the following year's program in which they hoped to expand IRISE to more classrooms. A proposal was submitted to the faculty that would expand class size to be on a par with other classes and reintegrate Latino and other students while maintaining 40% African-Americans in each IRISE classroom. Five White and African-American teachers from the staff were trained to teach these classes.

The issue of tracking and segregation was raised again as the IRISE proposal sought to expand students' time in IRISE classes. A revised proposal to the plan was to group IRISE students together in both core academic classes (language arts/social studies and math/science), thus mixing less with non-IRISE students during the day. The controversy resurfaced at a Restructuring Council meeting where the proposal was being addressed. Eve, an African-American assistant principal and a proponent of the new plan, explained to the Restructuring Council, "Without mincing words, sending a student from one classroom where the curriculum is particularly tailored for African-American students who have not historically achieved and sending them to another non-IRISE classroom, is setting them up to fall through the cracks."

Objections were raised surrounding "institutionalizing" segregation patterns at the school. In the Restructuring Council meeting, Peter said, "It seems like this plan is going to further institutionalize segregation. Now it could very well be that the success of directing education to kids who traditionally have really slipped through the cracks overrides that, but I'm concerned about that." The Restructuring Council agreed to support the new IRISE proposal with further discussion about the impact of linking core classes and it was headed to the faculty and grade-level families by the end of the school year.

At the end of the school year, the staff as a whole reviewed their students' standardized test scores and found that while all groups of students showed improvement from the previous year, African-American and English Language Learner students showed the least amount of improvement. The principal brought the data to the faculty meeting for discussion. As the teachers geared up to apply for BASRC membership, they planned to focus reform efforts on the achievement of those underperforming groups. The IRISE program, particularly its instructional practices focusing on African-American students, was one of the pieces of the reform. While it would lose its structure as an African-American-students-only intervention, its new incarnation involved more teachers using African-centered instructional strategies along with other pedagogical strategies.

The success of the pilot program was never formally evaluated; one of the original teachers pulled out; and the later incarnations of the program differed from the original proposal. Yet the efforts to address equity and underserved students of color remained central at Chavez. Teachers in different groups continued to debate the "right" way to address the needs of their diverse student population and work to close the achievement gap.

CONFLICT APPROACHES

At Chavez, teachers not only acknowledged that conflicts existed at their school; they expressed collective responsibility for them and at times embraced their differences in a public and vociferous way. While not always satisfied with their community responses to conflict, and frustrated by the lack of resolution, especially when it came to deep dilemmas about equity, teachers still actively engaged in struggles about beliefs and practices that resulted in changes in individuals and the school as a whole.

Conflict Ownership

Chavez teachers "owned" conflicts in their midst, assuming collective responsibility in addressing their differences. They overtly confronted each other, engaged in public debates and arguments, and raised difficult concerns with each other. They reflected on and evaluated problems together and critiqued their ongoing work in efforts to make changes. Through inquiry sessions surrounding their reform work, as well as during reflective meetings about their school site plan and standardized test scores, the faculty questioned their practices. Further, through activities with groups like Project Respect, the staff critically reflected on their differences (racial, sexual orientation, class, etc.). The goal of such critical reflection was change in the organization and in teachers' beliefs.

Teachers' collective capacity for self-critique and their commitment to schooling for social justice brought them to confront the fact that they were not reaching African-American students. They criticized their pedagogical, curricular, teacher hiring, disciplinary, assessment, and counseling approaches with this student population, along with their own racial awareness. In this way, they were able to discuss the IRISE initiative, and ultimately introduce the new program. This in turn opened up a multilayered discussion about the goals of desegregation, equitable distribution of resources, and the impact of teacher expectations on student achievement. Ultimately, the faculty exposed the dilemmas of trying to support a targeted racial group within a school whose mission is integration.

Similarly, they owned conflicts about teacher collaboration, confronting one another about not living up to their group norms and expectations. The eighth-grade team engaged in multiple activities to generate and reflect on group norms of accountability. Teachers exposed tensions of autonomy within collectivity and sought ways to accommodate individuality while still maintaining responsibility to team goals. The eighth-grade team took on multiple strategies to make public this conflict and discuss their differences. Rather than avoiding or suppressing such conflicts, Chavez teachers were outspoken about differences of belief and practice.

Norms and Practices of Collaboration and Consensus

Chavez teachers' norms of collaboration encouraged strong subgroup and individual affiliations that openly acknowledged diversity. Their conception of collaboration highlighted individuality and an acceptance of difference, which included, as Ben, a teacher/reform coordinator, said, "a nurturing and recognition of . . . individual styles and priorities . . . and space for dissent." Staff members acknowledged that there were different "camps" on school issues, openly discussing conflicting beliefs and practices. For example, while the eighth-grade team struggled to define what it meant to be a "family" with accountability to one another, they still supported the notion of individual autonomy, recognizing a tension in their practice about, as Gary said, "what extent to accommodate individuals to do their own things."

Demographic heterogeneity also contributed to a community that acknowledged divergent values and practices. Teachers could not easily ignore the questions of racial conflict raised by either their diverse student or adult populations. School activities that encouraged discussion of racial differences (about both teachers and students) meant that conflicts would be exposed. For example, a discussion about hiring practices at Chavez turned into debates about the meaning of affirmative action as teachers acknowledged the importance of a staff reflecting the racially diverse student population. Further, by hearing from his colleagues that teachers of color were not feeling supported as well as they could be at Chavez, Jake, a White teacher, gained new insights and came to change his perspective.

Chavez's carefully structured consensus decision-making procedures created opportunities to hear divergent perspectives, raise questions, honor dissent, and elicit competing proposals for change. At each of the meetings I observed where the faculty undertook this procedure, a number of teachers introduced objections that the community addressed. Facilitators acknowledged that these were important concerns and encouraged responses. Other teachers sometimes seconded the objections, or task forces were generated to think further about the concerns or develop co-proposals. When Max, an intern new to the school, was facilitating a faculty meeting and called for a vote, Jake responded, "Consensus doesn't work that way. We need to address the objections."

Even when dissenters finally agreed not to "block consensus," they wanted their objections noted in the meeting records. Ben explained that the consensus structures allowed "healthy expressions of dissent." He continued, "I think that in allowing people to disagree while at the same time not sabotaging or subverting something, [and the fact] that that's a respected place for people to be, is really important." While teachers diverged on multiple levels at Chavez, they did share a unity about the purposes of schooling. The divergence and conflicts arose within the context of this shared ideology.

Ideology

The teachers shared a critical ideology about schooling as a site of struggle for social change. Teachers identified their role as transformative agents. If their values challenged schooling as it existed, then continual struggle, the exposure of inequity and difference, had to be at the center of their work. Thus conflict became inherent within the community and was embraced as positive community behavior (e.g., a capacity for "getting real," a challenge to the "status quo").

Further, because Chavez's ideology is outside the mainstream (trying to create a schooling environment that is transformative or liberatory), there are no prevailing models or blueprints. Therefore, teacher conflict is further exacerbated as teachers struggle with competing conceptions of how to construct such a school. There is more to fight over within the school about approaches to reaching this end. As teachers collaborate to invent something new, they run into more conflict. For example, they chose IRISE as an experiment finding that they would have to debate whether this was the "right" way to go, because no formula exists for creating an equitable school.

Self-reports of Conflict "Avoidance"

While I found that Chavez teachers owned conflict, at face value many responses to the survey and interviews indicated that the teacher professional community was "conflict-avoidant." Teachers reported on the survey that they tended to avoid conflict (3.28) slightly more than embrace it (3.06) (where strongly disagree = 1; strongly agree = 5). They also tended to disagree with the statement "When we disagree about teaching, we openly discuss our differences" (2.37). How, then, can I claim that Chavez teachers embraced conflicts openly?

If the community finds itself avoiding rather than embracing conflict, what do they mean by that? Is it that they could not resolve their problems rapidly or that their expectations for exposing conflicts were so high that they were quite critical when their attempts fell short? I argue that the Chavez teacher community was highly critical of its ability to embrace conflict openly because they often exposed deep dilemmas that were not easily solved and also because their remarkable self-consciousness about conflict made them sensitive to sweeping issues aside. Teachers at Chavez identified confronting conflict as "getting real" and prized it as a goal. They often chastised themselves and the school for "sweeping things under the rug" or "avoiding conflict." Chavez teachers developed a low tolerance for leaving conflicts hidden or underexplored.

Conflict-frames, Solutions, and Mechanisms

Let's unpack the problem and let's see what is at the essence here and is this in fact the problem? Is the solution, in fact, appropriate to the problem? Have we done enough work on framing the problems and defining the problems? It's easy

to find a simple solution to a simple problem. It's more difficult to find a simple
solution to a complex problem. And maybe there is no simple solution. Maybe
the solution is complex, multi-layered, and shifting.
                                                        —Ben, Teacher/Reform Coordinator

Chavez teachers may have been particularly dissatisfied with how they resolved conflicts because they framed or defined disputes as complex, multilayered, and often ambiguous, which made it hard for them to be easily "solved." As Ben described in the quote above, the capacity to understand the meaning of problems may lay hidden below the surface and thus simple solutions may not be easily found.

Peter explained this process of exposing the multidimensionality of some conflicts as "peeling back an onion. There's layers and layers and layers." Ben articulated an example of this layered analysis when he framed the IRISE conflict in the following ways:

There are layers to the IRISE conflict. I guess there are larger . . . sociocultural layers. You can talk about inequities in society: racism, maldistribution of resources, etc. And then the ways that those get expressed in the institution of public education in the school. For example, the overrepresentation of White teachers and administrators, White middle-class norms and practices and the ways that they get expressed in the institution. Then I think there's the organizational or political [layer], which is the act of allocation of resources and the decisions that get made (which programs are funded, which programs aren't funded specifically in this school). And then the interpersonal conflict—different kinds of styles in groups, race, gender, sexual orientation—and the way that they get played out. And then [there's a layer] of intrapersonal identities, goals, assumptions, guilt, and expectations. All of those [layers impact] the battle that goes on . . . from being in this kind of a heterogeneous environment where conflict is being surfaced on a regular basis.

Many teachers expressed similar multidimensional analyses of the IRISE conflict in public settings. Teachers framed the IRISE debates as pedagogical conflicts over reaching African-American students, as resource conflicts over student loads and equitable distribution of funds for African-Americans, as racial conflicts between teachers, and as institutional disagreements about desegregation.

Most unusual was the teacher community's capacity to identify the institutional dilemmas that lay behind some of their conflicts. The teachers demonstrated a capacity to expose ambiguities and dilemmas of competing values that pervaded their educational environment. For example, they examined institutional dilemmas over segregating underperforming African-American students while fostering integration, and accommodating individualism amid community.

Because Chavez teachers saw conflicts as multidimensional, and often as rooted in deep institutional dilemmas, they developed a particular approach to solution-seeking. Rather than seek a single "best" solution, they developed ways of dealing with conflicts that were more like ongoing experiments with temporary solutions that needed to be constantly managed and renegotiated. Shawna, director of Project Respect, explained the school's conflict-framing and solution-seeking as "very postmodern thinking. There is no absolute truth, but rather we construct the truth. So then we are left with, what are the effects of our thinking through a certain lens? What expectations do we bring? What menu of options opens up from this?"

Chavez teachers approached their conflicts as chances for experimentation. In response to conflicts over collaboration, Chavez teachers tried multiple forms of teaming and shared decision-making structures. In a single year, the eighth-grade team alone revisited their group norms, rewrote them, called a meeting with administrators to discuss disputes, engaged in reflective process meetings with Project Respect, and changed leadership.

They were willing to try and to abandon more experiments because of their openness to the ambiguity of the conflicts. Thus, they tried a limited experiment in having two African-American-only classrooms for a year. Chavez teachers recognized that there was no perfect "solution" to these conflicts; they saw drawbacks to "segregating" a part of their population, while seeing the potential benefits. The IRISE "pilot" was portrayed as an experiment that would be attempted, evaluated, and changed where necessary, rather than conceived of as the one best solution.

Ongoing restructuring efforts at the school site and experimentation in decision-making procedures were strong components of Chavez's history. They developed an academy system, which they later rejected midyear. They then moved to the grade-level family system. Within grade levels they developed pods and quads for interdisciplinary teaming. Special education teachers experimented with various models of inclusion and team teaching. Project Respect generated the "praxis groups," which supported staff and teachers' collaboration in an experimental setting. They continually revised their meeting procedures and also created more time to meet as a whole faculty. At times though, this solution-seeking stance may have also resulted in wrong turns, frustrating dead-ends, and a propensity to judge harshly their ways of coping with conflict.

The repertoire of mechanisms to address conflict fostered public debate about values and practices at Chavez. Chavez's mechanisms tended to make public teachers' disagreements, and gave permission to teachers to deliberate collectively on organizational and institutional concerns. As a result, their professional discourse included normative debates about equity, and the responsibility of communities to individuals and individuals to communities.

The faculty had structures where concerns were raised, proposals made, dissenting opinions voiced and addressed. Teachers could formally make proposals to the faculty or engage in more personal explorations of differences in the setting of a praxis group. A remarkable number of ongoing evaluations and structured critical reflection (SB 1274, protocols, praxis group, Project Respect survey, School Improvement Plan reviews, etc.) enabled teachers to confront each other over the school's shortcomings in whole-faculty and small-group settings. Project Respect and other professional development work encouraged open and confrontational moments within the school day and beyond. Peter described how the array of venues enabled Chavez teachers to openly manage their conflicts:

> My sense is people do put things out because we have a number of
> structures for that. We have these family meetings. We have a pretty
> good meeting structure format. We have our faculty meetings and
> restructuring days. Then we have the Restructuring Council and we
> have a way to get things taken there and addressed. So there's a
> way to get things out and because it's been there for a while and
> there are enough people that have been practicing it, the new people
> can pick it up and follow along with a fair amount of ease. . . .
> Because we have a history of shared decision-making, people say,
> "O.K., my voice does count. Because I can make decisions and have
> an effect on the decisions made here, I should speak up."

This teacher identified multiple structures that enabled teachers to "speak up" and have their "voice[s] count." Further, Peter recognized a culture in which teachers felt a degree of agency in making changes. "I can make decisions. . . . If teachers didn't think their opinions mattered and they could have a say in it, then why would they bother trying to change things?" It is still important to note that other teachers, particularly teachers of color, reporting in a survey conducted by Project Respect, said they did not feel heard.

The principal, Julie, also played a role in the professional community's experience with conflict. Her openness toward conflict was noteworthy. "Conflict," she said, "does not have to be bad. If schools become stagnant, then they're not really always looking at what can we do better. Conversations about conflicts can create new ways of thinking and new ways of doing things." Thus Julie openly engaged in exploring conflicts in front of and along with the staff during formal faculty meetings.

She solicited divergent opinions and practiced a shared leadership style with both teachers and parents. She created a culture in which it was encouraged to risk dissent and expose disagreements with colleagues. She brought the student data about meeting the needs of their diverse students to the faculty to explore. She exposed a problem in the community and the faculty's responsibility for it, and openly struggled with the staff about ways to address it. She also brought resources, such as professional development from Project Respect, to the faculty to enable airing of differences, development of knowledge, and exploration of new practices.

The principal identified her leadership role as fostering conflict exploration among teachers and supporting them to manage their conflicts with one another. The principal's tendency to hand over conflict resolution to the teacher community removed a commonplace structure for channeling conflict away from teachers. Such confidence in the faculty fostered greater ownership among teachers and less deference to administrators.

In cases of conflict between teachers, she hoped to, as she put it, "empower teachers to be part of the solution. . . . I kind of leave it up to the staff person, that they have to take responsibility." This was seen in the case of the eighth-grade team that had called her in to discuss one team member's accountability for collaboration. The principal transferred back the conflict to the teachers, explaining that they needed to come to common agreements and hold each other responsible.

CONFLICT OUTCOMES

I turn next to the outcomes that resulted from Chavez's conflict stance. These outcomes address changes that occurred at the individual, community, and schoolwide levels. While creating a stressful environment for teachers, Chavez's conflict stance fostered diversity within their community and a potential for ongoing inquiry and organizational change.

Individual Experiences

Conflict took its toll on the faculty. Ongoing critique and an openness to conflict produced stress and frustration among Chavez teachers. Teachers explained that ongoing debates, especially about issues of race and equity in schooling, at times made Chavez a difficult place to be. The workplace was full of conflict.

On a five-point scale, Chavez teachers reported that "the level of conflict at my school increases my stress level" (3.58). Teachers of color (4.03) particularly identified higher stress levels than Whites at Chavez (3.03).[4] Teachers also attributed a history of teacher turnover at Chavez to excessive conflicts and frustration with colleagues.

Many Chavez teachers displayed enormous disappointment with colleagues for not holding up their end of teaming responsibilities. In response to conflicts over teachers' accountability to teaming, one teacher on the survey wrote that there was "much bitterness, anger, and frustration from teachers who feel like they must 'police' others" (Achinstein, 1997). Others, like Kati at an eighth-grade family meeting, expressed rage at colleagues who they felt "were not doing right by the students." Conflicts over issues of race and equity raised "a lot of pain and guilt" among colleagues, said Jake.

The high level of dissatisfaction with conflict resolution at Chavez left many teachers disillusioned with their school's change process, calling it "a superficial embrace" of conflict. Teachers who found Chavez avoiding or leaving unresolved conflicts about race or collaboration were responding to deeply complex struggles that were not easily resolved. For some, like Carla, an eighth-grade special education teacher, continually opening up difficult conflicts was like "exposing a painful wound" that would not heal. Some teachers reported that they had confronted conflicts in the past but were tired of getting no response, or just tired of the continual battle.

Some teachers pulled back from participation, describing actions as "shut down" because of "pointless" discussions of conflicts "where nothing really happens," as Samuel put it. For some, this sense of burnout and frustration had made them consider leaving the school. Tanya explained, "I'm getting very angry and I feel like I am not able to deal with that effectively. . . . I'm taking it in the classroom. I know this. And I refuse to do that. So that means I've got to stop, or quit, or whatever. I'll have to do that."

Community Ties and Borders

The conflict stance sustained diversity within the Chavez teacher community. Discernible "camps" were acknowledged around issues of teaching and school climate. These divisions were exposed and acknowledged in public debates over standardized test preparation, discipline policies, hiring teachers of color, teaming responsibilities, and the IRISE program. Such camps shifted depending on the conflict issue. The teachers' ability to form ties across traditional boundaries (race, gender, subject affiliation, etc.), while publicly discussing these differences, was notable.

Such a diverse community with an openness to conflict held implications for tolerance of difference and dissent within the collective. Chavez teachers such as Samuel, who challenged teaming, were given air time and sometimes accommodated. They maintained an "individualistic" status within the school, rather than being marginalized. Teachers who questioned racial integration during the IRISE debates also were encouraged. Community membership did not mean giving up subgroup or individual identity or beliefs.

The borders of the community were also quite open. Teachers identified students and parents as part of their community. This was seen as they discussed not reaching African-American students. They referred to them as "our students." Many teachers identified with the plight of marginalized students and their parents. The consent-decree tenets that each teacher signed also referred to teachers' responsibilities to every student in the school. Teachers were involved with the beyond-school community, soliciting parent involvement in schooling decisions. One teacher took a busload of faculty to the home community of students to understand more about their background. Parents were found in classrooms and governance meetings as well.

However, at times Chavez teachers struggled with maintaining their unity and clear borders as a teacher community. Recognition of divergent beliefs sometimes led teachers to feel less like a schoolwide teacher community and more like fragmented subgroups. Such an approach may have resulted in less collective action and collaboration as individuals and subgroups openly challenged shared goals. This was seen most clearly when Samuel, the eighth-grade teacher, openly resisted teaming and challenged accountability for collaboration. The end result was a less than unified team.

Organizational Change

Conflict played a role in impacting structural changes, reform efforts, and norms at Chavez. Teachers reviewing, critiquing, and challenging themselves, particularly on equity issues, meant there was a climate that supported organizational change. A sense of dissatisfaction coupled with a collective responsibility enabled the teachers to make these ongoing changes. Furthermore, the context of a common ideology with shared end goals enabled conflicts to become constructive, ultimately allowing teachers to coordinate school reform.

The conflict that arose around failing to meet the needs of their diverse students resulted in piloting the IRISE project, continued professional development on racial awareness, hiring more teachers of color, improved test preparation, and initiating a schoolwide reform effort to close the achievement gap. In the conflict over teaming, teachers acknowledged their responsibility and engaged in reflective processes, constructing new group norms, switching facilitators, and reaffirming ongoing commitments to upholding accountability goals.

Many of these changes were fragile. In both conflicts about collaboration and those of student concerns, the outcomes were still emerging as debates continued. Some teachers expressed frustration that the IRISE program was being reconfigured after its pilot year without systematically analyzing what did and did not work. The eighth-grade team continually had difficulty maintaining coordination. Their collaborative ties were relatively weak at times.

Yet Chavez teachers persistently monitored, challenged, negotiated, and renegotiated their beliefs and practices. This involved risk-taking and flexibility by a community that faced multiple challenges over time. The changes they did undertake were aimed at deeply engrained norms and practices in their community. By exposing dilemmas inherent in the dichotomy of individualism amid community, Chavez teachers questioned core values that defined the existing community. The community negotiated the boundaries of individualism within collaboration, as the eighth-grade team struggled with a "dissenter." Similarly, questioning the nature of desegregation and consent-decree mandates challenged values at the very foundation of the reconstituted school. Teachers deeply questioned the very premise of an integrated school by experimenting with IRISE and segregation patterns, while at the same time continually revisiting questions about the purposes of integration.

CONCLUSION

The Chavez teacher professional community is dedicated to collaboration, shared decision-making, collective inquiry, and progressive school reform. It is also a community that supports diversity in its midst. Marked by a social-justice mission and a commitment to changing the status quo, especially when it came to issues of equity in schooling and society, teachers at Chavez embraced struggle as a source of change and improvement. Thus engaging openly and actively with conflict became the norm and a positive community behavior.

In acknowledging their differences, teachers exposed numerous conflicts. Some arose over holding each other accountable to teaming and collaboration responsibilities. In an eighth-grade team conflict, teachers openly confronted each other on their responsibilities to the "family." The conflict was identified as multifaceted: a problem of clashing communication styles, an organizational problem of enforcing team accountability, and an institutional dilemma of balancing individualism and community. Multiple attempts were made to address the conflict through meetings, reflective processes, and changes in group norms and leadership. Some teachers were more optimistic than others about the team's ability to balance individualism and collegiality. But the team attempted to openly acknowledge the tension of autonomy amid collaboration, and make a space for their differences.

The community also faced conflicts over how best to meet the needs of their students of color. The IRISE debates depict exploration of contrasting values, goals, and practices over how best to reach African-American students at Chavez. Introducing an African-centered pilot program for African-American students raised much controversy. The issue was framed as a resource conflict by some. But those same teachers, and many more, also identified deeper organizational and institutional conflicts about race, expectations, standards, tracking, and even social change. These conflicts, debated in the faculty meetings and expressed in multiple interviews, opened up conversations about how teachers should teach, schools should be structured, and even society should be changed. The IRISE program was piloted, revisions were instated, and a schoolwide focused effort around issues of equity was established. The conflict was not "resolved," though, and discomfort with the dilemmas of fostering equity through schooling still remained. Debate would continue about the best way to meet the needs of the diverse student population.

Chavez teachers explored and at times embraced conflicts. They acted as critical colleagues, reflecting with one another about problems of their school, exposing differences of belief and practices, and working to fundamentally change schooling. Teachers owned responsibility for the problems and differences in their midst. Their collaborative practices fostered dissent and divergent thinking, allowing exploration of conflicts. Their embracing stance allowed for public and vocal debate among colleagues. The broad repertoire of mechanisms for public reflection and critique fostered open disagreement. The community's multidimensional conflict-framing practices drew attention to organizational problems and institutional dilemmas at the heart of many conflicts.

Such an embracing approach to conflict sustained a level of diversity within the community, respecting dissent and individualism among teachers, and also sparked a potential for organizational changes to meet the needs of students. New ideas were introduced to the community through conflict. New structures and strategies were continually experimented with as colleagues addressed their differences. Change became the norm. Teachers assumed that they needed to struggle for the best way to teach and the best schooling practices. They allowed their conflicts to change themselves and their school. They made the changes internally through self-reflection and externally in schooling structures that they found necessary to create an equitable education for their students.

Yet at times this embracing of conflict and ongoing change also created a stressful and frustrating environment for many teachers. Chavez was a place full of strife. It was also a place that continually exposed some intractable dilemmas that would never be resolved, thus exacerbating a sense of frustration. This took a toll on teachers.

Finally, such conflictual norms meant that teachers often struggled with the difficult balancing act of maintaining unity amid their differences of beliefs and practices. In many ways Chavez teachers demonstrated a difficult tightrope walk. It was a community respectful of its diversity, open to dissenters and strong subgroup affiliations. It maintained open borders of discussion. Yet it was also a community of teachers that attempted to achieve collective goals. The teachers struggled, and paid a price, to balance diversity within unity.

NOTES

1. All participants were given pseudonyms to maintain confidentiality. Direct quotations were taken verbatim from participants.

2. All quantitative references in this chapter represent mean Likert scale values drawn from my teacher survey. Unless otherwise noted, the scale ranged from 1 to 5 where 1 represents "Strongly Disagree" and 5 represents "Strongly Agree." The "n" for Chavez was 33 or 79% of certified staff. Unless otherwise noted, all subsequent references to survey means are from this survey (Achinstein, 1997).

3. I used teacher narratives and documents to reconstruct events for the first part of this story about the IRISE conflict, which occurred in the year before my study. For the second half of the story, I was able to observe meetings, conduct interviews, and collect documents on events during the course of my study.

4. Where $p = \leq .05$. The "stress" factor was constructed from three survey items. Each had a factor loading of at least .61. To see individual items, refer to Methodological Appendix.

CHAPTER 4

Conflict Amid Community

The Chinese character for conflict is made up of two different symbols superimposed. One symbol identifies danger while the other signifies opportunity (Hocker & Wilmot, 1985). Conflict is often considered perilous in the literature on community, but it also provides an opening up of possibilities, a generative source for change and renewal.

Both Washington and Chavez are teacher professional communities as assessed by self-identification and researchers' criteria. Both schools scored as strong communities by scales developed in terms of opportunities to learn, collegial support and collaboration, collective problem solving, and a culture of experimentation and innovation (McLaughlin & Talbert, 1996; Talbert & McLaughlin, 1994). Further, both met Louis et al.'s (1996) criteria of shared norms and values, reflective dialogue, deprivatization of practice, collective focus on student learning, and collaboration.

Conflict was absent in these criteria and self-identification of professional community, yet conflict was alive and well in both cases. This finding raises a number of questions. What can we learn from the two schools about the nature of conflict amid community and how teachers manage their differences? What lessons can we draw from the role of conflict in community in relation to change? How, as the Chinese character symbolizes, can conflict pose both danger and opportunity for communities?

First, we learn that rather than being aberrant behavior, conflict is inevitable and embedded in the very norms of community building. Second, we find that different schools approach similar conflicts in very different ways. They differ in how they own, frame, and manage conflict; practice collaboration and consensus; and even think about conflict in relation to the purposes of schooling. Third, and most important, these different stances toward conflict matter in terms of school reform goals. How each community approached its conflicts impacted the lives of teachers, the bonds and boundaries of the community, and ultimately the school's capacity for change and learning.

Through a cross-case discussion, this chapter explores how teacher communities deal with conflict and implications for their potential to reform their schools. It examines the nature of conflict amid teacher communities, both its dangers and its opportunities, and concludes with reflections and implications for the theory and practice of teacher professional communities.

CONFLICT AND COMMUNITY FORM
AN UNEXPECTED MARRIAGE

Contradiction and conflict not only precede unity but are operative in it at every moment of its existence . . . . There probably exists no social unit in which convergent and divergent currents among its members are not inseparably woven.

—Simmel, 1955, p. 15

Although the teacher professional community literature promises greater consensus and shared values, these cases reveal that community and conflict formed an unexpected marriage. Both communities were born in conflict. At Washington, the restructuring reform that first introduced interdisciplinary teaming generated intense conflict and divisions among colleagues, resulting in some teachers leaving the school. Chavez's teacher community was initiated in a legal battle and tumultuous reconstitution. Communities are born in conflict because collaboration and unified efforts challenge teaching cultures and norms of privacy, independence, and professional autonomy, as well as the disjointed or "loosely coupled" nature of schools as organizations (Little, 1990a; McLaughlin & Talbert, 1993; Weick, 1976).

Both communities remained in conflict over time as they continuously engaged in collective reflection, questioned existing practices, and uncovered competing interests. Being a "community" raised expectations about collective accountability that continued to generate conflict in both schools, as colleagues negotiated the competing demands of collaboration and individual autonomy as evidenced in the two schools' eighth-grade teams. Teams at both Washington and Chavez faced conflicts when a single member challenged accountability for teaming responsibility. Dan, at Washington, labeled a "resister," confronted other teammates about the burdens of collaboration. Similarly, Samuel, at Chavez, challenged his "family" by not endorsing the group norms and practices. Both examples illustrate the tensions between the individual and the collective as teachers move to more collaborative configurations.

Collaboration and consensus—critical elements in building community—actually generated conflict. Not only did the teacher professional communities experience multiple conflicts, but the conflicts were promoted by the core norms and practices that define teacher communities. Whereas, historically, teachers could retain their private and diverse beliefs behind closed classroom doors, innovations that supported collaboration opened up such differences to scrutiny and often resulted in conflict. Structures that fostered teacher-teacher collaboration, such as schoolwide or grade-level teaming, made public collective decisions about practice. Collaboration, particularly as colleagues examined their practice, "generate[d] heat as well as light" (Little, 1990b, p. 188).

At both schools, the search for consensus paradoxically raised the level of public dispute. The adoption of consensus-based decision-making meant the faculties had to come to agreement on values and practices. Thus, differences among colleagues had to be addressed. At Washington, a consensus decision-making process used at the introduction of their teaming reform initiative generated a dispute between "resisters" and "reformers." At Chavez, a consensus process, over piloting the IRISE program, allowed for public dispute over approaches to addressing African-American students at the school.

By airing diverse perspectives in a collective setting, by raising expectations for teacher input, and by allowing teachers to debate what and how to do schooling, these schools generated new conflicts *because* of their commitment to creating community. Thus conflict was neither the antithesis of community nor aberrant. Rather, it was an essential component of community. As the Simmel epigraph above suggests, conflict forms a marriage with community.

FROM AVOID TO EMBRACE: A CONTINUUM OF CONFLICT STANCES

Given the presence of conflict amid community, how did each community respond to its conflicts and what were the results of such approaches? This section explores a continuum that demonstrates how differently communities manage their conflicts. Exploring a continuum of conflict stances is important because these stances shaped the nature of reform outcomes in the two schools. They resulted in different kinds of changes at the individual, community, and ultimately school levels. Thus understanding the spectrum of conflict responses is critical to appreciating different reform outcomes.

While past research painted a unified picture of communities either devoid of conflict or rapidly able to achieve consensus, these two cases demonstrate that communities manage conflict quite differently. Overly unified images may reflect the interest of administrators and managers who favor smoothly running school cultures. Such "effective" cultures may emphasize rapid consensus around administratively managed outcomes and thus underplay conflict (Deal & Kennedy, 1982; Purkey & Smith, 1983; Rosenholtz, 1989). But in the Washington and Chavez schools, teacher communities approached conflicts in contrasting ways.

The experiences at the two schools helped me define significant distinctions along a continuum of conflict stances. The continuum (see Figure 4.1) represents a spectrum of conflict stances or characteristics of how communities manage conflict. Toward one end of the continuum lies an *avoidant stance*, identifying a community's ability to rapidly absorb, exclude, or transfer conflicts and thus maintain a unified community and stable school environment. Toward the other end of the spectrum lies an *embracing stance*, which involves a community's acknowledging, surfacing, and owning conflicts by critically reflecting on their differences of belief and practice in efforts to foster fundamental change in the school.

Four dimensions or distinguishing features that represent a community's beliefs and practices around managing conflict further characterize each stance. *Conflict ownership* describes the ways that a community acknowledges or excludes conflicts. *Norms and practices of collaboration and consensus* identify the generalized rules of conduct and structures of teacher-to-teacher interaction. *Ideology* of schooling defines the framework of shared values held within a teacher community. *Conflict-frames, solutions, and mechanisms* identify how a community defines, makes sense of, and ultimately sorts through options to manage differences.

In general, Washington's stance toward conflict remains closer to the "avoidant" side of the continuum and Chavez's stance closer to "embracing." This contrast is best exhibited by their differing approaches to conflicts about student concerns. Washington teachers sought to blame students as the source of the problem, transferring the conflict outside of their own teacher community, thus maintaining solidarity among "us" in opposition to "them." Ultimately, by identifying "problem students," like Lani, at the center of their conflict, Washington teachers strengthened existing discipline policy while leaving their own practices and attitudes unquestioned. The rare voices of dissent were often marginalized or excluded. Such was the case with Eliza, the special education teacher, who raised the conflict between teachers' espoused commitment to teaching "all students" and their practices that missed an at-risk 30% of students.

In contrast, teachers at Chavez responded to the problem of sending too many African-American students to the counseling office and low student achievement by debating different beliefs and practices in public. They confronted one another and sought to find ways to change. In their subsequent public, schoolwide debates about IRISE, an African-centered program, Chavez teachers articulated their differences about allocation of

FIGURE 4.1. *Continuum of Conflict Stances*

	AVOIDANT STANCE		EMBRACING STANCE
Conflict Ownership	*Avoid/Exclude*	←——→	*Acknowledge/Embrace*
	Exclude, rapidly absorb, or transfer conflicts		Acknowledge, solicit, and own conflict by critically reflecting on differences of belief and practice
Norms and Practices of Collaboration and Consensus	*Unanimity/Unity*	←——→	*Dissent/Diversity*
	Collaboration is highly unified, with low levels of individual or subgroup identification		Collaboration involves diversity or heterogeneity of affiliation and beliefs with individual and subgroup identifications
	Consensus means unanimity and harmony with low dissent		Consensus includes opportunities for alternative views and active dissent
Ideology of Schooling	*Mainstream/Congruent*	←——→	*Critical/Counter*
	Mainstream ideology about the purposes of schooling—to socialize students into current society; teacher's role is socialization		Critical ideology about the purposes of schooling—to build critical thinkers and actors to transform, rather than reproduce, current society; teacher as change agent
	Inside school ideology congruent with dominant messages from the environment		Inside school ideology in conflict with dominant messages from the environment
Conflict-frames, Solutions, and Mechanisms	*Unidimensional*	←——→	*Multidimensional*
	Clear, agreed-on, and single definition of conflict and solution		Multiple levels of analysis, ambiguity, and complex conflict-frames and solutions sought; ongoing experimentation, adjustment, and redefinition of problems
	Limited repertoire for public debate while active informal mechanisms privatize conflicts		Broad repertoire of mechanisms for public debate of conflicts on beliefs and practices

resources, philosophies of integration, and conceptions of equitable practice. This led to experimentation and the piloting of the IRISE program, and continued discussion about teaching for equity.

The Washington teacher community tended to avoid or transfer conflicts outside of its borders, uphold highly unified norms of collaboration where consensus meant unanimity, espouse a mainstream ideology of schooling congruent with dominant messages from the environment, frame conflicts and solutions in unidimensional ways, and provide limited mechanisms for public debate. In contrast, the Chavez teacher professional community tended to acknowledge and at times embrace conflicts, foster dissent and diversity amid collaboration, espouse a commonly held but critical ideology of schooling, frame conflicts and seek solutions in multiple ways, and provide a broad repertoire of mechanisms for public debate.

The purpose of having a continuum is to represent variation. The two cases I studied fall on different places on the continuum, rather than at the opposite ends. It is often tempting to dichotomize, placing the cases at polar opposites of a continuum, but this would not represent the complexity of the similarities and differences between the two teacher communities. There were also times when the communities fell into a middle ground on the continuum, exhibiting simultaneous impulses of conflict acknowledgement and avoidance. This hybrid stance demonstrates some of the complexities of phenomena represented along a continuum.

In no way should communities be seen as static, fitting in one place on the continuum at all times. Because teacher professional communities vary and the same community changes over time, they may find themselves at different points along the continuum at different points of time. It is also possible that a group of teachers run the gamut of stances as they work through a single conflict, thus exhibiting multiple stances at the same time. The usefulness of such a continuum is not found in inserting teacher communities into a fixed formula, but in helping further explore and deepen understandings of diverse conflict stances. Next, I illustrate each dimension with examples from the cases.

Conflict Ownership: From Avoid to Embrace

The continuum depicts a range of responses to owning conflict. Toward one end are approaches that exclude, absorb, or transfer conflicts and at the other lie approaches that acknowledge, solicit, and at times embrace differences of belief and practice.

A poster on the wall at Washington that was used to promote "conflict mediation" for students read:

What to do when someone bothers you—

Ignore the person
Move away from the person
Ask politely for the person to stop
Tell the person firmly to quit it
Give warning and then get help
Count to ten

Tell a student conflict mediator or an adult that you need to do a conflict mediation

I was most struck by the first two directives. In many ways, they captured some of the adult responses to conflict as well—ignore and move away.

In contrast, Chavez teachers put a different sort of poster on their walls. To create a "safe school," where different sexual orientations and gender identities were recognized and not stigmatized, teachers posted pink triangles designating spaces to discuss difficult issues. Each teacher received a pink triangle poster as part of his or her professional development work focused on gay/lesbian and diversity issues sponsored by Project Respect, demonstrating that this was a safe place for diversity and that they were "allies." Allies believe that diversity enriches the school, will challenge stereotypes and slurs, and will create a safe atmosphere.

At a professional development meeting, a teacher described a name-calling incident when one student called another a lesbian. Whereas the teacher was initially hesitant to address the issue, a third student pointed to the triangle posted on the wall, the ally sign, and said that this is a safe place to talk about these difficult issues. The student referred to the triangle as she opened up a complex whole-class discussion on name-calling, gay issues, and heterosexism at Chavez.

These examples expose contrasting responses to conflict. One community found ways to suppress or transfer conflicts from its midst by projecting it onto other stakeholders. The other acknowledged ownership for conflicts. While both schools' eighth-grade teams had to deal with a single teacher objecting to collaboration, their opposing responses were striking. The Washington team labeled Dan a resister, found that the problem lay with him, avoided any discussion of different beliefs, and took the conflict to the principal to resolve. At Chavez, the team attempted to address the concerns collectively and publicly through reflection, and in so doing uncovered dilemmas of supporting autonomy amid community.

The two communities also dealt with student-related conflicts in contrasting ways. In Chavez's case, teachers talked of how "*we* are sending too many African-American students to the counseling office," identifying teachers' role in the problem. Chavez teachers went on to collectively debate teachers' practices and beliefs around meeting these students' needs, examining student achievement data, identifying an achievement gap, disagreeing over teacher hiring practices, discussing different equitable pedagogical strategies, engaging in professional development and dialogue about their differences, and ultimately experimenting with IRISE.

In contrast, Washington teachers attributed the conflict to "defiant" students and sought ways to exclude them. Rather than identify a discrepancy between their own vision statement and practice in reaching "all students," Washington teachers located the source of difficulties with "problem students" and sought ways to exclude them from the community. They undermined any dissenting viewpoints by calling for solidarity among teachers, asking, "Aren't we going to support our own?" Those who held different views, like Eliza, the special education teacher, expressed their differences privately or left the school.

While Washington's teacher community raised some conflicts, its norms of minimizing dissent and transferring conflict outside of its borders served to exclude other conflicts. In contrast, Chavez teachers acknowledged diversity of beliefs and practice, found space for dissent in a public arena, and at times critically reflected on, owned, and explored a variety of conflicts.

Norms and Practices of Collaboration and Consensus: From Unanimity to Dissent

> Ellen: *An approach has been implanted so we don't see the conflict. [The principal] uses the term* consensus. . . .
> Dan: *Yeah, we took those who disagreed and shot them.*
> —Washington teachers

> *I think that's one of the key aspects of collaboration . . . there's plenty of space for dissent here.*
> —Ben, Chavez teacher/reform coordinator

The norms and practices of collaboration and consensus mediated the two communities' experiences of conflict. The continuum illustrates a spectrum from unanimity (where collaboration is highly unified and consensus means no disagreement) to dissent (where collaboration involves diversity and consensus includes divergent perspectives).

Washington community with its tightly linked collaboration built an expectation of homogeneity and social cohesion. It also tended to have conceptions of consensus as harmony, unanimity, and, at times, conformity. Dissenters were defined as deviant or resistant to the community and therefore were to be excluded or marginalized. At the core of Washington teachers' conception of collaboration was a vision of a social web of relationships, or interpersonal ties of caring and a friendship between colleagues, that formed the bonds of stability. Many were best friends within a demographically homogeneous setting. There was a high level of interdependence and a low degree of individualism. Construing community as a close-knit web of friends based on commonality, homogeneity, and agreement meant that conflicts appeared as tests of loyalty and thus had to be transferred outside the borders.

Washington teachers' practice of consensus-based decision-making resulted in furthering this perception of total agreement. First introduced as a way to end conflict over their teacher reform, consensus really resulted only after dissenting faculty left. The withdrawal of resisters not only ended the conflict, providing consensus among those remaining, but sent a message to nonresisters about their fate if they were to challenge consensus. Similarly, the characterization of dissenters as having psychological deficits made the practice of disagreement pathological, or at least disloyal, community behavior. Furthermore, the practice of identifying the majority will and calling it consensus obscured a minority perspective. Their consensus practice sustained norms in which consensus meant unanimity. Thus they are situated closer to the unanimity/unity end of the continuum, identifying low dissent and highly unified norms and practices of collaboration and consensus.

In contrast, the Chavez community was more diverse, with loose collaboration, differentiation or heterogeneity, and individual and subgroup affiliations. Teachers identified multiple "camps" within the community, recognized racial differences among staff, and articulated divergent perspectives on teaching and learning. Further, the racial and ethnic diversity of the faculty affected the kinds and level of conflict experienced within its community. Chavez teachers' conception of diversity within community, their subgroup and individual identities, their expectations about divergent beliefs and practices, meant that differences and conflicts were accepted and oftentimes welcomed.

Here dissent and multiplicity of interpretations, perspectives, and voices were solicited and conflict was engaged as important to the functioning of the community. For example, the hiring committee was at odds about what affirmative action meant in terms of hiring more teachers of color. Teachers stated their conflicting interpretations, shared divergent experiences, and debated beliefs before agreeing on a policy. Tanya "got plain" in making her differences with Jake over hiring practices quite clear. Teachers of color also shared their experiences of feeling unsupported at the school and this perspective was news to Jake. Ultimately, these debates allowed the new hiring policy to address both ways to hire more teachers of color and ways to give them ongoing support once at the school.

The community's practices of consensus decision-making also encouraged dissent, objections, and time to address concerns. The practices of publicly dissenting and documenting different voices were seen in their collective meetings. Objections were raised when Chavez teachers discussed plans for a second-year IRISE program (to address African-American students) with a new configuration that would extend the amount of student time in IRISE classes and decrease integrated time with non-IRISE students. In a Restructuring Council meeting, Peter wanted to be sure to express his disagreement: "It seems like this plan is going to further institutionalize segregation. Now it could very well be that the success of directing education to kids who traditionally have really slipped through the cracks overrides that, but I'm concerned about that." The proposal, along with the objections, would be discussed further within the Restructuring Council and then taken to the whole faculty for discussion.

At times, such dissent, subgroup affiliation, and individuality made joint effort difficult at Chavez. Samuel's dissenting from the eighth-grade group norms made uniformity of practice across the grade quite difficult. Further, the original IRISE experiment, though agreed to by the whole school, was piloted by a few strong advocates. There were, in fact, issues of nonunity and lack of consensus at play in the school. Thus, Chavez is situated closer to the dissent/diversity side of the continuum.

Ideology: From Mainstream to Critical

> *It's not about changing society. It's about bringing these students' scores up. It's about meeting the goals of the district in raising test scores. We hope that by making the curriculum . . . coherent from kindergarten through eighth grade, the students will improve.*
>
> —Karen, Washington teacher

> *Education is an institution of change. Changing what? Changing the society, changing attitudes, changing issues of power, making social change, hopefully beneficial social change. [Generally,] people don't see it like that, my perception is that they see it more as a job and they're good people and they're helping to educate young people and these sort of platitudes but when it comes to helping them, educating them to do what? It's to maintain the status quo. . . . I see what education should be as liberatory; it's to challenge the existing social system and change it. Because it's evil and it's corrupt.*
>
> —Samuel, Chavez teacher

While dissent and diversity were the norm at Chavez, there was still a unity of commitment found in their shared ideology of schooling for social justice and equity. This shared ideology served as a common framework that united the community, while debate and dissent remained about the means for achieving such ends.

The continuum depicts an ideological spectrum from mainstream conceptions about schooling for socialization that are congruent with dominant messages from the environment to critical conceptions of schooling for transformation of society that conflict with local and national messages.

Ideologies of schooling shaped contrasting experiences in the two cases. As reflected by Karen's comment above, Washington teachers tended to uphold more mainstream notions of education, identifying school as a site to socialize students into the current society, and ultimately to serve as a stabilizing influence for society. This ideology aligns with reigning messages and models of schooling, thus diminishing conflict within the walls of the school.

In contrast, as reflected by Samuel's comments above, Chavez teachers tended to support a more critical view of schooling practices, a notion of schooling for social justice, and a transformative vision of the role of education in society. Such views challenged dominant (mainstream) conceptions in the environment and thus promoted acceptance of continual conflict. Chavez communities' ideology placed conflict at the core of the educational process. Their conception of their roles as critically transformative educators within a diverse community supports their approach to embracing conflict, upholding dissent, and exploring multiple perspectives. If the goal of schooling is to critique and change society, then the enterprise should be rife with conflict.

Furthermore, Chavez is linked to an ideology for which there are no prevailing models in the wider environment from which the community can draw. Chavez is trying to invent a different way of doing school—a socially just and transformative way. There are no current robust conceptualizations or determinate ways for conducting school in this way. Teacher conflict is further exacerbated as teachers struggle with competing conceptions of how to construct such a school. Having to invent a new way of schooling through collective work, within the context of counter pressure from the wider environment to reproduce current models of schooling, increased conflicts.

Frames, Solutions, and Mechanisms: From Uni- to Multidimensional Approaches

The continuum illustrates the range from unidimensional conflict-framing and solution-seeking to more multidimensional approaches. Washington teachers framed conflicts as distinct problems generating from one clear source, and thus easily solved. Conflicts were often seen as organizational issues to be addressed structurally, or as personality clashes to be handled individually, rather than as multilayered and complex institutional dilemmas that evade easy solutions. Thus what could have opened normative debates about teachers' beliefs and practices associated with challenging students was instead framed as problem children and a need for stronger disciplinary procedures (a solution that did not necessarily address the needs of "the 30%"). Intra-team conflicts over collaboration were seen as caused by resistant individuals or personality differences and resulted in switching team organization. These teachers found single solutions to their conflicts. These solutions, once implemented, were not easily abandoned.

Washington teachers took a more rational approach to school organization, one that fostered a sense of coherence in a world of ambiguity. When a single problem is framed, an overwhelming conflict may become more manageable and "solvable." Such a stance brings clarity and certainty to the often ambiguous and unpredictable culture of schools.

The Chavez teacher community framed conflicts as more multidimensional and ambiguous, identifying dilemmas that must be continually negotiated. Identifying multiple causes behind conflicts broadened the arena of debate from purely technical "problem-solving" to deliberation on a range of personal beliefs, organizational practices, and normative values. In framing conflicts as multilayered dilemmas, the community had to continually negotiate compromises. Such an approach resulted in ongoing experimentation, less defined "linear progress," and circuitous routes to change. For example, conflicts about students uncovered multiple layers, including pedagogical conflicts over reaching African-American students, resource conflicts over class size, and institutional dilemmas about race, equity, and desegregation. In this way, Chavez teachers uncovered dilemmas of competing values as well as organizational problems. Recognizing that there was no perfect "solution" to these intractable dilemmas of education, they chose to "experiment." Chavez teachers took a "let's try it and see" attitude to tension-filled situations. They accepted ambiguity and nonetheless tried to act as reasonably and thoughtfully as they could toward their preferred ends, rather than becoming paralyzed by the uncertainty.

Conflicts are addressed more informally . . . behind closed doors. You know, people don't want to make an issue of it because it's a confrontation.
                                                                —Shannon, Washington teacher

People do put things out because we have a number of structures for [address-
ing conflict]. . . . People say, "O.K. my voice does count. Because I can make
decisions and have an effect on the decisions made here, I should speak up."
                                                        —Peter, Chavez teacher

Conflict Mechanisms. Beyond frames and solutions, the repertoire of
procedures to raise and address differences in belief and practice are also
vital for understanding a community's experience with conflict. Such
mechanisms may include formal consensus-based decision-making procedures in faculty meetings, informal conversations behind classroom
doors, forays to the principal's office, and so forth. Different structures and
procedures engage teacher communities in very distinct kinds of conflict
discourse. Some mechanisms may privatize conflict, limiting collective participation, while others may foster public exploration. Some processes
provide multiple points of entry through an array of forums for voicing
diverse perspectives, while others are more limited.

Washington's formal structures of addressing conflict allowed teachers to raise some conflicts publicly (primarily organizational/technical
problems like strengthening discipline procedures) and rapidly come to
consensus. Other conflicts, such as intra-team disagreements, were brought
to the principal for resolution, rather than having teachers negotiate. Their
extensive private interchanges, such as over inter-team competition and
jealousy, often removed debate from a public arena. They privatized their
conflicts in order to evade a sense of disloyalty or breaking of personal
friendship ties. This privatizing of differences reinforced their avoidant
stance and diminished public disagreements.

In contrast, at Chavez, an array of mechanisms to address conflict
brought debate into the public arena and allowed multiple points of entry
for teachers. Their ongoing processes of critical reflection and self-evalua-
tion (through protocols, surveys, program reviews) at full staff meetings
allowed Chavez teachers to confront each other over the school's shortcomings. Professional development work encouraged open and confrontational
moments within the school day and beyond. For example, "consent-decree
week," during which faculty discussed issues of teaching for equity; "praxis
groups," in which teachers engaged in reflective discussions about the connection between theory and practice; and "dialogue" groups that addressed
conflicts between teachers and students and teachers and teachers, particularly over issues of race, all provided a public forum for conflict. These contexts offered staff an opportunity to learn the language of difference and
conflict under the supervision of Project Respect facilitators versed in conflict mediation and diversity training. These settings also connected reflec-

tive conversation to teachers' public expectations for change in practice. Thus they moved from inquiry "navel gazing" to action.

Principals' Approaches to Conflict. The site administrator, a traditional mechanism for conflict resolution, played an important role in how teacher professional communities negotiated their conflicts in these two cases. The principals' conflict stances and leadership styles were connected to the level of conflict ownership experienced within the teacher communities. The administrators exhibit contrasting approaches to conflict, as reflected by their comments below:

> Conflict does not have to be bad. If schools become stagnant, then they're not really always looking at what can we do better. Conversations about conflicts can create new ways of thinking and new ways of doing things. (Julie, Chavez principal)

> I'm conflict-avoidant. (Ted, Washington principal)

Washington's principal, Ted, admitted being personally conflict-avoidant, which echoed the faculty's stance. Paradoxically, while personally avoidant, Ted tended to absorb teacher conflicts, taking them from teachers and then resolving them rapidly to sustain stability and harmony among teachers. Ted explained that he wanted to diminish teacher conflict that might disrupt collaboration and school reform goals.

Ted's leadership style was more traditional than that of Julie, Chavez's principal. At Washington, many conflicts were brought to the principal for resolution, which contributed to the teachers' lack of ownership in negotiating their differences. Teachers deferred to the principal as final arbiter of conflicts, removing the conflict from public debate among the teacher community. When team members disagreed, Ted intervened to switch teachers onto different teams to avoid conflicts. When Dan, the eighth-grade team member, challenged his obligation to a team, the principal again was involved.

The Chavez principal's shared leadership style made authority relations more lateral than hierarchical, putting conflict ownership in the hands of teachers. While Julie was called on to settle some teacher-teacher conflicts, such as when the eighth-grade team called a meeting with administrators about accountability to teaming, her approach was to turn back responsibility for resolution to the teachers involved. Julie's tendency to hand over conflict resolution to the teacher community removed a commonplace structure for channeling conflict away from public debate among teachers.

Furthermore, Chavez's principal publicly engaged in critical reflection about her own and the school's shortcomings, opening up opportunities to hear divergent perspectives and multiple solutions. She brought the test scores that demonstrated a racial achievement gap and the question of what to do to the faculty. Julie brought Project Respect and other support providers and resources to the faculty as they began to explore different beliefs and practices around teaching for equity. Ultimately, Julie identified conflict as an opportunity for exploring new ways of thinking and doing school—a conflict-embracing stance. She was not only the leader but also a member of the inquiring community, participating in exploration of differences, sharing her own opinions and also creating the contexts for others to share their divergent beliefs. Thus her leadership facilitated conflict exploration.

Lack of Union Role in Teacher Conflicts. One traditional mechanism for addressing conflict among teachers is the union. The relative absence of a union role in either of the two cases is worth noting. While both schools are union schools, each having one school-building representative to the local association, the union played a minimal role in the conflicts that emerged between teachers. During the course of my study at Washington, there was only one mention of the union in relation to teacher collaboration and conflict (when Dan threatened to call the union on his team), and one reference to a teacher strike around wages approximately 15 years earlier. At Chavez, no teacher mentioned the union in relation to teacher collaboration and conflict.

With 80% of the teachers in the United States belonging to union affiliates, union presence in teachers' professional lives seems almost universal (Bascia, 1994, p. 1). Yet what explains the lack of union presence in the teachers' lives in this study? Furthermore, one would anticipate a major role for unions in relation to conflict in schools. Why not in these cases?

The answer lies with the congruence or lack thereof in values between the local teacher community and the values in the union. In the case studies, the teacher communities' identity as professional colleagues superseded their union membership. First, unions are perceived to focus on salary and working conditions, and less so on matters of teaching and learning. It therefore makes sense that the issues that these teachers were focusing on did not bring in the union. The union may have been seen to perform an important but limited function in terms of bread-and-butter issues. Second, the union may be seen as an important player in terms of adversarial relations with administrators, and others with different power levels, but not with their own peers with whom they were constructing a new identity. Conflicts that arose between colleagues were handled in arenas other than union mediation—they were handled in teacher-to-teacher interactions within private and public meetings, or sometimes with the help of principal interventions. Therefore, the significance of the more local context (within-school) may have kept conflict from moving to the level of a districtwide professional organization, which was perceived as outside their own community boundaries. Bascia's (1994) work on unions concurs with this finding, identifying the key to a union role linked to a match with school values.

OUTCOMES OF CONFLICT STANCES

The current reform rhetoric on teacher professional community says that individuals are said to benefit as they diminish isolation, uncertainty, conservative teaching practices, and alienation through developing more satisfying working relations. The community of teachers is supposed to grow from its collaborative practices, forming a supportive, unified, and resilient context. Ultimately, the school as an organization is said to have greater potential for reform and ongoing learning, as teachers coordinate schoolwide change initiatives, engage in ongoing inquiry and renewal together, focus collectively on the needs of their students, and align goals and practices.

This section examines what outcomes actually did result from each community's responses to conflict. The two cases reveal a surprising lesson, challenging the current reform rhetoric that equates unified (read "low-conflict") communities with renewing and learning organizations. Instead, the cases disclose that the community that avoided conflict may have been more satisfying for individual teachers, but served to limit fundamental change and sustain homogeneity. The community that tended to embrace conflict may have generated more stress, but also created a greater potential for ongoing organizational learning and diversity amid its community. What's good for school reform can be stressful for teachers and create community relations that are not as harmonious as the literature says. Conversely, I found that the teacher community that would be highlighted as successful in the literature, because it was harmonious with less conflict, actually limited its potential for the kinds of fundamental change and ongoing renewal needed for school reform.

A Continuum of Conflict Outcomes

The continuum of conflict stances demonstrates that communities approach conflict in very different ways. They differ in how they own, frame, and manage conflict amid their collaboration.

Why do the different ways that communities handle conflict matter? The answer is that different stances toward conflict matter for school reform outcomes about which researchers, reformers, and practitioners care. How communities manage conflict shapes teachers' individual experiences, the kinds of borders around the community, and most important, schools' capacity for organizational learning.

The cases illustrate a range of outcomes that fall along another type of continuum, one that includes three dimensions: (1) individual experiences of teachers that result from conflict management; (2) community ties and borders that change relationships within and beyond the teacher community; and (3) organizational changes in structure, reform efforts, norms, and practices at the whole school level that may result in learning (see Figure 4.2).

At one side of this continuum are outcomes that result from an avoidant stance. These outcomes highlight individual teachers' sense of satisfaction with conflict management, the tightly bonded nature of community ties, the less permeable borders that define membership, and the maintenance of existing norms and organizational stability. At the other side of this continuum are outcomes from an embracing stance. While individual teachers experience frustration, stress, and burnout from high levels of conflict, the community promotes diversity and inclusiveness, and ultimately holds a greater potential for organizational change and learning. In general, the Washington teacher community tended toward the outcomes of the avoidant stance, and the Chavez teacher community tended toward the outcomes of the embracing stance. What follows is a discussion of conflict outcomes as illustrated by examples from the two cases.

Individual Experiences: From Satisfaction to Frustration

Rather than the agreeable emotions of care, support, and empathy offered by advocates, teachers in both communities I studied identified frustration and anger associated with conflict they experienced from their collaborations. While most community advocates concentrate on positive emotional states, many remain blind to what David Hume termed the "disagreeable passions" (Hume, 1948, cited in Burack, 1994). Teachers in this study were angry with their colleagues when different approaches to practice, students, and career expectations were played out in an atmosphere of perceived support and care. Teachers at both schools expressed anger at colleagues for not actively participating in collaborative activities, for not holding their end up as professionals, and for betraying group norms. Yet overall, the outcomes of the two schools' conflicts resulted in different experiences for teachers as individuals.

FIGURE 4.2. *Continuum of Conflict Outcomes*

	AVOIDANT STANCE		EMBRACING STANCE
Individual Experiences	*Satisfaction*	⟵⟶	*Frustration*
	Sense of satisfaction with conflict handling; positive reports of community and conflict		Sense of frustration, burnout, and stress due to conflicts
Community Ties and Borders	*Bonded/Exclusive*	⟵⟶	*Diverse/Inclusive*
	Highly bonded social ties; homogeneity within community		Individual and subgroup identities upheld; heterogeneity of beliefs and participants fostered
	Rigid or impermeable borders that form barriers to outsiders		Fluid social arrangements, open boundaries, sometimes fragmentation
Organizational Change and Learning	*Stability/Static*	⟵⟶	*Fundamental Change/Learning*
	Solutions result in maintenance of existing social relations and norms		Conflicts result in questioning core norms, organizational change, potential for organizational learning

Washington teachers' ability to achieve rapid consensus in the face of conflict led to a stronger sense of satisfaction with the community's responses than did Chavez's. Their unidimensional conflict-framing served to bring clarity and certainty to a largely confusing educational world. Thus teachers could ask the principal to reorganize team membership when individual "personality differences" surfaced. Teachers could strengthen discipline policies in response to "problematic children." At times, they reaffirmed their ties by transferring conflicts outside of their boundaries onto "resistant teachers," who leave, or "problem students." Ultimately, these teachers identified that they were happy with how little conflict they experienced and how rapidly they were able to achieve consensus. They associated this success with maintenance of strong personal ties, as demonstrated by this interchange between Val and Ellen:

Val: ... people like each other here now.
Ellen: An approach has been implanted so we don't see that conflict.
[The principal] uses the term—*consensus.*

Alternatively, Chavez teachers identified a higher level of stress and frustration associated with conflict with colleagues than did Washington teachers. Because Chavez teachers often exposed the multiple layers of conflict, they became angry and discouraged when what they thought would be a simple decision turned into a conflict, which then turned out to be an unresolvable dilemma. Thus their discussion of sending too many African-American students to the counseling office moved from a procedural issue to one that uncovered resource, racial, institutional, pedagogical, and philosophical issues about desegregation and equity in society. These problems are not as easily solved; rather, they rely on the faculty's living with greater ambiguity, an acceptance of agreeing to disagree, and an ability to move forward in the face of uncertainty. Such a stance toward ambiguity is no easy feat and produces anxiety.

Furthermore, ongoing experimentation and organizational changes that challenged core beliefs and practices also took their toll on Chavez teachers. As teachers continuously opened up deep differences that resulted in rapid reform and restructuring, faculty experienced burnout. Some described becoming bitter about working with colleagues and others chose to leave or to work part-time. Chavez, with its public controversies, was a stressful context in which to work.

Community Ties and Borders: From Bonded to Diverse

Conflict shaped the relations within and without the communities by delineating the nature of *ties* among members, and demarcating the *borders* for insiders and outsiders to the community. While advocates promise a sense of identity and belonging from community building, they talk less about exclusionary practices that can impact teachers, students, and the broader school community. Yet, as Simmel (1995) and Coser (1956) found, conflict can be crucial in fostering internal group solidarity through construction of a common external enemy. "The group as a whole," Simmel explains, "may enter into an antagonistic relation with a power outside of it, and it is because of this that the tightening of the relations among its members and the intensification of its unity . . . occur[s]" (1995, p. 91). Nias et al. (1989) agreed, writing about a professional community that defined groupness by "finding an enemy" (p. 93) or locating the opposition. Alternatively, other communities may use conflicts to continually embrace "outsider" perspectives and membership, expand their borders, and reshape the bounds of thinkable thought (Chomsky, 1989).

   Ties Within Community. These two cases illustrate that the conflicts that arise during collaboration may limit or create space for diverse identities within the teacher professional community, and exclude or include a broader school community. In terms of ties within the community, Washington teachers experienced more unity within community as a result of their conflict approaches. Low levels of dissent and a conflict-avoidant stance promoted strong ties and a sense of unanimity. Washington teachers tended to agree more with the statement "after a conflict we quickly try to reunite as a faculty" than did Chavez teachers (Washington 3.29; Chavez 2.76). For example, Washington teachers identified strong consensus about teaming after resisters left.

   In contrast, at Chavez, different camps and diverse perspectives were still visible even after decisions had been made about how to handle a conflict. This was seen in discussions of the IRISE program in which teachers identified their divergent stances on desegregation, even after committing themselves to experiment with the program.

   Chavez's stance also meant that a sense of wholeness or unity was often difficult to identify, creating the potential for fragmentation at the community level. At times, teachers identified much more with subgroup than with whole-school affiliation. Divergence of beliefs, though, was situated within the context of a commonly shared ideology at Chavez. Thus, disagreements did not question shared values about the purposes of schooling. But disagreements did allow for exploration of multiple perspectives on how to address the problems of schooling, as well as foster individual and subgroup identification.

   Negotiating Borders. Conflict also offers a key occasion for negotiating borders, the lines that delineate inclusivity or permeability, both within the boundaries of the community and in relation to those outside such as students or parents. The two cases illustrate contrasting kinds of borders because of their differences in conflict ownership and collaborative practices.

   Washington's teacher professional community defined its border by identifying unified membership in opposition to "others." As a result of its conflict stance, the Washington community helped to determine its "us" identity in opposition to "them," whether they were "resistant teachers," "problem students," or "problem parents," all of whom "didn't belong." Teachers resistant to the collaborative reforms were not just described as excluded but (albeit jokingly) eliminated—"We took those who disagreed and shot them." This pattern was echoed as teachers sought to "support their own," defending their borders by removing or isolating challenging students.

While Washington teachers maintained solidarity among colleagues, they may have done so at the expense of unwittingly labeling "problem students," effectively excluding 30% of the children. Thus the high walls that formed their community borders kept out a large group of students for whom they were responsible. The teachers also built walls between what they saw as their commonness in contrast to parents and the neighboring community. Parents were often blamed for the problems of their children. Few parents were actively involved in shared decision-making or the daily life of the school. Few of the mostly White teachers lived in the neighborhood or identified with the racially diverse working-class community.

In contrast, Chavez's responses to conflict defined a more diverse community with more open boundaries that were inclusive and expanding. Teachers' identification with multiple and shifting subgroup affiliations both within (in terms of pedagogical "camps" and subject and grade-level teams) and outside of school (racial, ethnic, and political affiliations) made borders permeable and less clear. Chavez teachers often identified with traditionally marginalized stakeholders such as students and parents. They included students as part of their community, particularly when they took ownership for not reaching African-American students. They used "we" language to include students within the community— "we are not meeting our students' needs." They continually solicited the voices of parents and outside stakeholders by going into the community beyond the school and inviting them to participate in schoolwide decision-making. Thus the borders of Chavez expanded and opened to the larger community.

Organizational Learning: From Learning for Harmony to Learning for Inquiry

While this chapter discusses three dimensions of conflict outcomes—individual experiences that result from conflict management; community ties and borders impacted by conflict; and changes in structure, norms, and practices at the whole-school level that result in organizational learning— perhaps the most crucial outcome is the last one. Organizational learning is highlighted by community advocates, and yet underconceptualized in relation to conflict. Exploring the connection between conflict and learning calls into question the promises of organizational renewal claimed by teacher community advocates. The different conflict stances—whether a community owns or avoids conflict—really matter in what and how teacher communities learn and schools reform.

A Surprising Lesson About Conflict and Learning. These cases disclose the surprising lesson that the professional communities currently highlighted as successful in the literature because of their low levels of conflict may be less generative, less capable of learning for fundamental change, than more conflict-ridden ones. In contrast, the community that openly embraced conflict demonstrated a greater potential for achieving the reform outcome of fostering organizational learning for ongoing renewal. I call this a surprising lesson because we'd like to believe that harmony is more desirable than conflict and that strong ties are preferable to weak ones. Yet these cases reveal an important story about the relationship between harmony, strong community ties, and organizational learning.

Kinds of Organizational Learning. Researchers advocate fostering teacher professional community and collaboration as a vehicle for school reform and ongoing learning (Johnson, 1990; Lieberman & Miller, 1990; McLaughlin & Talbert, 1993; Rosenholtz, 1989). The cases demonstrate that conflict is essential to learning and change. But what kind of learning and change results? To understand the complexities of the two cases in this book, I distinguish between learning that tends to maintain the stability and *harmony* of the organization and learning that results in ongoing *inquiry* and fundamental changes. Learning that results in adaptive or incremental changes fosters stability and harmony. Here, an organization seeks to adjust to its environment while maintaining core norms, practices, and relations. In what Argyris and Schön (1978) call "single-loop learning," members of an organization respond to changes in the environment by detecting problems they can correct and may undertake incremental changes while maintaining the norms and practice already in place.

In contrast, learning that results in generating new insights in order to change behavior or routinely questioning values that guide organizations falls into the ongoing inquiry and fundamental change category (Huber, 1991; Rait, 1995). Argyris and Schön (1978) identify this kind of inquiry as "double-loop learning," which "consists not only of a change in organizational norms but of the particular sort of inquiry into norms described as learning" (p. 22). Such inquiry fosters "a new sense of the nature of the conflict, of its causes and consequences, or of its meaning for organizational theory-in-use" (theory that governs action) (p. 11). McLaughlin and Talbert (2001) similarly define this kind of learning in community as one that reexamines rather than reaffirms institutional norms.

In both teacher professional communities that I studied, organizational learning resulted from the conflict stances. But the kinds of learning were quite different. While Washington's learning maintained stability and harmony, Chavez's learning promoted inquiry, continual reflection, and a climate for ongoing school change.

Washington's Learning for Harmony. Washington teachers' conflict avoidance, their interpersonal connectedness, and their consensus-oriented ideology contributed to fostering learning for harmony and organizational stability. Their preferred value of harmony tended to reinforce core norms and suppress opportunities for inquiry and ongoing organizational change and learning. For example, in Washington's conflicts about students, teachers strengthened their discipline practice, leaving unexplored teachers' expectations for students, differences of teachers' beliefs, and a potential to change teacher practices around addressing the needs of "the 30%." In another conflict, teachers switched teams rather than explore their different professional beliefs.

Conflict could have served to alienate individuals within the community, to destabilize it to the point of not producing collective work, or ultimately fracture the community into polarized subgroups. Instead, at Washington the teachers were able to reaffirm their bonds and maintain their practices. In the setting of multiple changes in their context—demographic shifts in student population, changing demands of accountability from the district and the state, and new school reform initiatives—such stability served a vital function. The social harmony experienced among staff supported ongoing collaborative efforts, allowed for incremental changes within the organization, kept teacher retention high, and allowed the staff to rapidly come to consensus and move forward as a whole.

Static Settings and Groupthink. One of the dilemmas of such harmonious or stable communities is that while promoting positive outcomes, they also may become static or conservative settings with few mechanisms for reflection, change, or transformation. In underplaying dissent in favor of consensus, such communities limit inquiry and change. As Fulbright (1964) advocated, "Learn to welcome and not to fear the voices of dissent, where we dare to think about unthinkable things because when things become unthinkable, thinking stops and action becomes mindless." Washington teachers marginalized dissent through the construction of "others"—those deemed outsiders and often enemies of the community. They were often labeled deviants or heretics and thus marginalized or excluded from the group. Heretics are those who hold views that are beyond dissent, and their views are dismissed as personal deficits (Hargreaves, 1994). This was seen in the case of teachers resistant to teaming at Washington, and again with students who were considered "defiant." Constructing heretics limited the diversity of perspectives of the group as it dismissed deeply challenging views and limited the community's capacity for empathy as it distanced itself from "flawed" individuals.

Communities that foster a high degree of consensus without arenas for dissent easily fall prey to "groupthink." Groupthink, a term coined by Janis (1972), refers to going along with group decisions without questioning or allowing dissent (Fullan, 1993, p. 82). Fullan warns that groupthink is a danger of "hypercollaboration" (Fullan, 1993). Groupthink illuminates another meaning for the expression "the ties that blind," highlighting the restraining function of group bonds. Such groupthink limits an organization's capacity to grow and learn in response to its changing environment. Negative consequences of suppressing conflicts have been similarly documented by organizational theorists who found that concurrence-seeking and homogeneous groupings reduce innovation and the quality of decisions (De Dreu, 1997; Rubin, Pruitt, & Kim, 1994). The extreme consensus-seeking of groupthink is predicted to lead to collective rationalizations, stereotypes of outsiders, limited exploration of alternatives, and impaired decision-making, among other things (Turner & Pratkanis, 1997, p. 54).

Washington's closed community, tendencies to suppress dissent, and low degree of self-critique perpetuated a group reinforcing its own perspectives and biases. For example, by avoiding or leaving unexplored a conflict between the school's vision statement that "all students can learn" and teachers' daily practice of labeling and excluding, the staff at Washington inhibited their ability to change teaching and schooling beliefs and practices to address an underserved 30% of their student population.

Thus the very teacher professional communities currently highlighted as successful by the literature—those with shared values, high degrees of consensus, and strong bonds—may strengthen some values but be less generative or capable of learning for fundamental change than other more conflict-ridden or conflict-embracing ones. By excluding conflicts (leaving them hidden), rapidly absorbing conflicts (no exploration), or transferring conflicts onto outsiders, community members seldom challenged their assumptions and practices. Their unidimensional frames, primarily focused on individuals, limited opportunities for inquiry into collective norms. Their approach to dissent meant that challenging ideas, alternative perspectives, and new thinking were diminished. In exchange, they gained collective harmony and stability.

Chavez's Learning for Inquiry. Most current descriptions of communities find conflicts and approaches like those experienced at Chavez problematic at best, pathological at worst. Yet Chavez's conflict stance enabled the potential for the kinds of inquiry and organizational learning advocated by reform theorists. Conflict and diversity were situated as central to the working of the community, to its future growth and transformation. Their embracing stance toward conflict engaged the community in an inquiry process that explored divergent beliefs and practices of the community, owned responsibilities for conflicts, plumbed underlying dilemmas, and even questioned the organization's premises. In doing so, they created opportunities for both learning and fundamental change.

Conflict played a role in changing structures, reform efforts, and norms at Chavez. Chavez teachers' exploration of conflicts over race, student expectations, and teacher accountability enabled them to investigate their shortcomings in meeting the needs of African-American students and to develop new programs and avenues for inquiry. Their stance resulted in piloting the IRISE program; hiring more teachers of color; starting a teachers-of-color lunch forum; examining student test score and referral data; ongoing professional development around diversity, pedagogy, and reform; and changing teaching practices.

Their continual debates about collaboration and accountability brought the teachers to question their conceptions of individualism within community as well. This was evidenced during the eighth-grade team's process meetings, where they opened a dialogue about accountability that resulted in revisiting group norms. These represented the potential for sustained inquiry and renewal within the community.

At times, the teacher community engaged in a form of inquiry that challenged the core norms of the community. For example, questioning the nature of desegregation and consent-decree mandates challenged the very foundation of the reconstituted school. Teachers inquired into the very premise of an integrated school by experimenting with IRISE and segregation patterns within the school, while at the same time continually revisiting questions about the purposes of integration. While deeply engaged in conflicts, Chavez still maintained a high degree of consensus about the ideology of schooling. Without that framework of shared purposes, they might have been too conflictual to change. Within this context, though, Chavez teachers were endeavoring to challenge, negotiate, and renegotiate their beliefs and practices as a community.

Such an approach is vital to teacher communities interested in becoming communities of inquiry, engaged in ongoing reflection for the purpose of change. An inquiring community explores divergent beliefs and practices of the community; acknowledges and owns responsibilities for conflicts that may result; solicits multiple levels of analysis—often disclosing underlying dilemmas; and at times questions the organization's premises in order to change them. As communities collectively challenge their core norms and values, they create opportunity for fundamental changes (Argyris & Schön, 1978).

"Community is not about silent consensus," Bellah et al. explain; "it is a form of intelligent, reflective life, in which there is indeed consensus, but where the consensus can be challenged and changes—often gradually, sometimes radically—over time" (1985, p. 16). Reflection and conflict offer a community the opportunity for change. The ability to engage in critical reflection and openly explore dissent is vital to fostering a renewing and learning community. Critical reflection involves teachers in thinking, criticizing, and transforming the current conditions of work and schooling. It is a process of questioning "taken-for-granteds" (Louden, 1992) for the purpose of considering how certain practices and conditions might be changed (Tabachnich & Zeichner, 1991).

Certain skills and processes are necessary to engage in such critical reflection. It is not an innate practice; rather, teachers need to learn the language and capacity for critique. At Chavez, professional development opportunities and mechanisms that supported critical reflection (such as protocols or inquiry around data) served to produce a culture, teach a language, and provide the specific structures for ongoing learning and change.

Dissent—the voicing of alternatives and the challenging of the majority—offers a great stimulant for inquiry and organizational learning. As Nemeth (1989) found, "people will consider the issue from multiple perspectives, one of which is that posed by the minority. As a result, thought will be divergent in form" (pp. 100–102). Nemeth's study on minority dissent found that the quality of group decision-making and performance was raised through dissenting views. New types of learning are possible because dissent fosters divergent thought processes, opens up possibilities, and questions the previously unquestionable.

Tjosvold (1997) similarly documents research on group processes that shows how "through open conflict people combine and integrate their ideas to solve problems and strengthen their relationship. Conflict is essential to realize the benefits of collaborative work" (p. 26). The open dialogue of opposing views that makes cooperative settings productive has been characterized as constructive controversy (Johnson, Johnson, Smith, & Tjosvold, 1990; Tjosvold, 1985). Constructive controversy allows individuals to begin to doubt the adequacy of their own perspective and seek to understand one another more. Ultimately, this can lead to a higher quality decision and one the group is willing and able to collectively implement (Tjosvold, 1982; Tjosvold & Deemer, 1980).

Because schooling is a normative profession, rife with moral dilemmas and indeterminate solutions, conflicts provide an opportunity to analyze and explore different value choices to be negotiated and renegotiated during a change process. The free play of multiple perspectives and openness to disagreement foster such growth. Embracing conflicts in multidimensional ways enables dilemma-based thinking rather than the traditional leap to "problem fixing" that schools frequently undertake. Exploring the institutional and normative bases of conflicts enables exploration of what is worthy of conflict, what some of the systemic barriers to change are, and where school people can take responsibility for change. Such a stance promotes educational renewal and ongoing learning.

Fragmentation and Fragility. But while Chavez was potentially a more responsive organization than Washington, a word of caution is necessary. Chavez's approach also created a climate for sustained conflict that could promote fragmentation of the community or burnout of its teachers over time, thus undermining organizational learning. Chavez's stance created a stressful working environment, full of uncertainties. This learning for inquiry also served as a destabilizing force in the community. Continuously debating fundamental beliefs and constantly changing practices made Chavez's reform efforts fragile and community ties tenuous. Deconstructing what were perceived to be shared values without always having solutions for where to head promotes a sense of ambiguity and unease.

Inquiring communities may promote change, but they also provoke anxiety. High teacher turnover, dissatisfied teachers, and fragmented reform efforts were some outcomes associated with Chavez's inquiring stance. Thus, I stress the greater probability or potential for learning, while remaining somewhat cautious given that I do not have evidence over a longer term.

An optimal level of conflict within groups may need to be identified for it to be productive. Examining relations between conflict intensity and group performance, Walton (1969) and De Dreu (1997) found that when conflict is too high, stress can limit decision-making and reduce diverse thinking. But if conflict is too low, there is no necessity to look for new ideas.

Moreover, those communities that openly engage in conflicts, currently assumed to be pathological, may be more healthy and have a greater potential for undertaking the processes of fostering inquiry, organizational learning, and ongoing renewal that we associate with positive reform outcomes.

FUTURE DIRECTIONS FOR THE THEORY AND PRACTICE OF TEACHER PROFESSIONAL COMMUNITIES

This chapter has discussed how conflict is inevitable within teacher communities and, more importantly, the fact that how a community approaches its conflicts matters for teachers, communities, and an organization's capacity for learning. The two cases challenge conceptions of what renews teacher communities and schools, placing conflict at the center rather than the periphery of community practices. Reconceptualizing conflict is central to a deeper understanding of how teacher communities exist in practice. This section includes reflections from the two cases of conflict amid community and offers some thoughts about future directions for the theory and practice of teacher professional communities.

Conflict and Hope

It is time to reframe notions of conflict. While previously considered a dysfunctional or pathological aspect of communities, conflict reflects a more hopeful and healthy future for communities and schools. To engage in conflict and question one's beliefs with the possibility of deep change is a fundamentally hopeful act. Conflict offers a teacher community the opportunity to look at schools as they are and see what they can become. It offers a context for inquiry and organizational change.

In the conflicts discussed in this book, teachers began to ask which students are not learning and they began to challenge one another about their practices and ultimately to make schoolwide changes. This is a hopeful act; within it lies a sense of collective agency.[1] There is an understanding that in working through differences, teachers can improve the opportunities of their students and their broader school community. It is an act of hope to delve into a conflict with colleagues, an expression of belief in one another to make a difference. "When conflict is brought to the surface," explained one Chavez teacher, "that's when it becomes real. It will go somewhere." To engage in conflict is a sign that the fundamental relationship and purpose are worth the struggle. If we rethink conflict as a hopeful sign, viewing it as inevitable and necessary, then when we see it or experience it we can appreciate its connection to growth and learning.

Future Directions for Research

This more hopeful image of conflict within community calls for new avenues of research. This positive reframing demonstrates a need for further study that includes conflict in the examination of teacher professional communities. It also highlights the significance of ideology in shaping conflict stances, and thus a need to reexamine differing frameworks of educational values held by communities.

Discourse on Conflict. A changed mindset about conflict amid community means reexamining the current discourse on conflict. Conflicts are often interpreted as "unprofessional" within teacher communities (as personal differences to be resolved outside of faculty rooms, as resistance to be over-come, or as deficient community behavior). What my study highlights is that debate, dissent, and disagreement are part of the repertoire of professional discourse in teacher communities; that is, conflict discourse should be added to current conceptualizations of teacher professional communities. If con-flicts are a natural, inevitable, and at times fruitful part of teacher profes-sional communities, then conflict discourse—deliberation about beliefs and values, dissent, and disagreements over practices—can no longer be rele-gated to the domain of "unprofessional" or "dysfunctional" talk.

Most research literature on teacher communities lacks a conversation on the existence of conflict, let alone the role that collaborative norms may play in generating conflict. Emphasizing teachers' shared values and con-sensus that should result in expressions of caring and belonging, teacher community advocates often miss examining the professional discourse of debate, dissent, and conflict among colleagues that could result in school reform. Researchers, policymakers, and practitioners alike must incorpo-rate this missing conversation about conflict into their work on and in pro-fessional communities.

New research studies must systematically analyze the inevitable coun-terpart to collaboration—conflict—as well as the diverse ways that communi-ties approach conflict. Further research is needed to confirm the relationship between conflict and organizational change. Because my study examined only a short period in the life of two teacher communities, more comprehen-sive, longitudinal studies will prove important in discerning the long-term impact of conflict approaches. How does the handling of one conflict im-pact later responses? Are the organizational changes sustainable over time? Such research would hold important implications for both teacher commu-nities and the change literature. More research is also needed to examine the costs and benefits of contrasting conflict approaches. Is it necessary for teach-ers as individuals to experience tension and discomfort for the organization to generate a potential for fundamental change? An important question that my study did not address extensively was the relationship between the teacher communities' experiences with conflict and student's experiences. How are they linked? What is the impact of teachers' stances toward con-flict on student learning?

Ideology Examined. While past researchers and advocates of teacher community identify the importance of having shared values and commit-ments, they often ignore the content or ideological substance of such val-ues (Westheimer, 1996, 1998). Yet these ideologies impact a community's experience with conflict and frame how teachers act. A community that shares beliefs about schooling for socialization of children in the service of social stability will underplay conflict in search of harmony, whereas another community upholds conflict as crucial to their transformative vision of schooling. These two communities experience conflict, learning, and change quite differently. These ideological differences matter in terms of how teachers teach, how schools are organized, and possibly how society is ultimately shaped.

Yet research on community has often underplayed such ideological differences. For example, Sergiovanni (1994) described the importance of communities' bonding around shared values or philosophy, while finding "the subject matter of this focus and clarity may well be secondary" (p. 100). He finds both Christian fundamentalist schools and Coalition of Essential Schools successful communities and "the specific undergirding educational philosophy may not be the key" (p. 100).

However, not all teacher communities are alike. Nor are all theories and values of communities worth sharing. Teachers, individually and collectively, hold values that shape their practice. Further, values outside the schoolhouse walls also permeate and interact with those found inside the walls. The content of a teacher community's ideology, especially as it pertains to values about education, schooling, and students, does matter. These conceptions frame how school is enacted.

The ends that result from certain theories may be less desirable than others. For instance, the ideology behind a Christian fundamentalist school may be exclusion of those who do not agree with or deviate from church canon, whereas a Coalition of Essential Schools' community may encourage members to be reflective, inquiring, and even challenging of core practices. How teachers teach, students think, and the community interacts are deeply affected by these contrasting theories of education. Ultimately, we must inquire into these theories, find out what they are, and ask which are worth sharing in educative communities.

The two communities I studied held different ideologies about schooling, which resulted in contrasting experiences with conflict. Mainstream ideologies served to foster stability and align with dominant societal expectations about schooling, which diminished a role for conflict at Washington. "Here, education is used," as Bernbaum (1977) states, "to maintain conditions for 'social integration based on consensus, where individuals behave in ways appropriate to maintain the society in a state of equilibrium'" (p. 18, cited in Kanpol, 1992, p. 4).

In contrast, more critical educational values, like those at Chavez, that challenge the way schooling "is supposed to be," that call into question institutional norms of schooling for socialization, put conflict and struggle at the core of teachers' work. Kanpol (1992) describes the role of conflict with such a critical conception of schooling.

> Conflict . . . was not in need of a quick fix but viewed as necessary for revolu-
> tionary change from a stultifying and all too slowly predictably changing sys-
> tem. Put in the context of teacher work, content taught, teacher relationships
> to authorities, to peers and the wider culture have definite political overtones
> and must be seen as such if schools are to act as sites of social critique, conflict,
> struggle and transformation. This becomes the politics of teaching. (p. 5)

Whether the teachers in a community uphold mainstream or more critical educational values matters in their responses to conflict and ultimately in how they teach and enact schooling.

Conflict is still a very difficult thing for teachers, full of stress and anxiety. Yet it is a site for learning and change. Teachers need a common commitment to abandon their comfort zone to delve into difficult differences. This takes a level of will and moral urgency found in certain ideologies of schooling. Given the current inequities that are promoted within schools, particularly as they relate to a racial achievement gap seen in both of my study schools, an ideology of schooling that remains dissatisfied with the current state of affairs has greater potential for promoting democratic and equitable outcomes for all students. I take up this question of the ideological content of communities and what ideologies are worth sharing further in the last chapter.

Rather than assuming that any common ideology makes for a healthy community because it is shared, researchers should examine the content or nature of such ideologies and what goals they support. Thus the theories about the purposes of schooling held by communities must be further examined.

Future Directions for Policy and Practice

Beyond research, expanding the discourse on conflict within community holds significant implications for policymakers and practitioners. In particular, this more hopeful understanding of conflict calls for expanded roles for teachers and administrators as they engage in moral deliberation and exploration of professional differences. It also means that policymakers and practitioners will have to provide supportive systems and structures for such conflict exploration to occur. Finally, practitioners will want to examine the nature of their community borders as they build bridges or create barriers to the broader school and local communities.

New Professional Roles. If discourse on conflict is to be considered part of the professional community, then teachers' and administrators' professional roles also have to be reconceptualized. New directions include an enlarged role for both kinds of practitioners.

Conflict discourse offers an expanded conception of teachers beyond that of technicians or problem-solvers—to be morally deliberative beings, managers of dilemmas engaged in exploring purposes and contexts of teaching. Such activities involve teachers in asking hard questions of themselves and colleagues, and surfacing their own beliefs and confronting others on theirs. Teachers would identify it as their role to confront themselves, each other, and even society at large.

Such a conception of professionals is similar to Aronowitz and Giroux's (1991) notion of teachers as transformative or "public intellectuals." They see the notion as a basis for "teachers to engage in a critical dialogue among themselves." It allows teachers "to undertake the language of social criticism, to display moral courage, and to connect with rather than distance themselves from the most pressing problems and opportunities of the times" (p. 109). This is an expanded notion of professionalism, one that includes embracing social criticism and conflict. Chavez's case may best help us understand this expansion of professional discourse. The teachers' norms of self-critique, exploration of dissent, and overt conflict-embracing stance resulted in public confrontations about values and practices. Their meetings included negotiation and debate about individual, organizational, and institutional conflicts.

Similarly, the principal's role needs to be reconsidered. Traditionally, principals are seen as the final arbiter of conflicts between teachers. Conflict resolution among staff is often framed as the principal's professional responsibility. This study calls into question the principal's role and authority relations at the site level and how they impact conflict ownership. How can principals act as leaders, modeling conflict ownership, while encouraging teachers to engage in professional disagreements? How can principals, at times, hand conflict back to teachers to engage in productive differences? How can a principal be both a member of a community engaged in inquiry and conflict exploration and the facilitator of this process?

Louis and Kruse (1995) identified key features of principal leadership about conflict, which involve encouraging forums for teachers to discuss differences, reinforcing community values as a way to manage conflict, and demonstrating a willingness to live with ambiguity (pp. 221–222). I would add to these: modeling critical self-exploration and vulnerability; fostering openness to different perspectives; handing conflicts back to teachers and thus not becoming the final authority; and providing multiple structures, resources, professional development, and practice in inquiry and shared decision-making as key features of leadership about conflict.

Professional development will be needed to support teachers and principals in examining the nature of conflict and ways of addressing it collectively. Professional development and opportunities for individual and collective inquiry are critical in identifying individuals' beliefs in order to help them articulate "what's worth fighting for" (Fullan & Hargreaves, 1991). Supporting the development of a language and a climate for conflict discourse is also needed. Promoting greater understanding of the political context of schooling so educators are not unaware of the conflictual nature of school interactions will contribute to these ends as well. Further, principals should be supported in rethinking leadership as empowering the authority of teachers to collectively engage in the professional discourse of conflict.

Conflict Systems and Structures. New languages and cultures alone will not necessarily result in communities that learn and grow from their conflicts. Structures, processes, and systems to manage conflict in constructive ways also matter. This study captured differences in the nature of mechanisms to address conflict and how they shaped the way conflicts were framed and owned, and solutions were sought. Soliciting conflict and managing it in ways that foster learning and growth require carefully constructed systems and structures. Otherwise, conflict can remain at the interpersonal level, erode the sense of community, or explode outward to chaos. Further, in the absence of conflict systems, teachers fall back on the only ways they know of handling differences. For example, at Washington, where disagreement was interpreted as disloyalty to friends, teachers lacked a system for depersonalizing conflict and addressing it in other ways.

Different systems impacted the level of participation among community membership, the public or private nature of conflict, the depth of inquiry, the spectrum of perspectives sought, and processes for promoting organizational change. For instance, Chavez's conflict systems included procedures to solicit divergent beliefs and generate conflicts through a repertoire of public and semi-public forums. Their consensus decision-making procedures fostered dissent, and their inquiry and data-analysis systems created opportunities for critical reflection on practice. The staff's work with Project Respect provided opportunities to listen to alternative perspectives and different voices in the community, to connect beliefs with practice, and to push teachers to take action. Washington's procedures often allowed for the maintenance of trusting relationships among teachers by structuring interdependent collaboration, extensive time working on teams, and opportunities for private conflict resolution.

Policymakers and practitioners alike should consider the support systems that foster and inhibit a capacity for teachers and schools to address conflict. If advocates want to foster a capacity for teachers to have critical professional discourse, then supports are necessary to create a climate in which practitioners solicit, explore, and address conflicts. Such supports would include extended time together, opportunities to examine data and student work, mechanisms that provide for conflict discourse and debate, administrators' roles in supporting teachers to engage in public debate, and opportunities to reaffirm relationships.

This last point about sustaining relationships is key. Structures that promote conflict exploration without tending to collaborative ties limit the group's capacity to learn or take action collectively. What Deutsch (1973) calls promotive interdependences or cooperative relationships create the context for productive conflicts and decision-making that promotes common understandings, commitments, and active collaboration in implementing change (Amason & Schweiger, 1997). Thus structures and systems to support a collective orientation and mutuality are vital in transforming a conflict into a constructive controversy for a teacher community. Opportunities for authentic joint work (Little, 1990a) on meaningful issues—such as examining student work and attention to caring adult relationships in school (Noddings, 1992) by keeping teachers together over time, providing common spaces, and explicitly addressing the complexity of collegial ties in professional development—may attend to promotive interdependence.

The findings of my study also challenge some reform-minded policies and practices advocating collaboration and consensus. Policy initiatives that put teachers in groups and expect them to learn and grow disregard the complexity of the collaborative process and often ignore the inevitable conflicts that will arise. In this way, many reforms leave practitioners unprepared and with few supports for addressing conflict. Thus policies should reflect the difficult nature of such reforms, highlight strategies to address conflicts, and accommodate the dilemmas inherent in community-building initiatives. Further, if organizational change and renewal is the goal of some community-building policies, then policymakers must consider the role of dissent and disagreement in learning. Policymakers may want to consider the significance of fostering a healthy climate of disagreement and dissent.

Policies then must allow for the time it takes to both build and sustain relationships, to engage in deep dialogue about differences, to allow conflicts to surface, and ultimately to solicit different perspectives and ways to manage these differences. This means that reform "results" take a form different from just improved student achievement or a single vision of a highly bonded teacher community. They take the form of a resilient and inquiring professional community. It also means that it often takes more time than most current policies allow.

Rethinking Borders. This study also highlights the fact that how teacher communities negotiate their borders matters greatly for teachers, students, and the broader local community. The nature of borders and the identification of outsiders should be included in practitioners' conversations as they articulate the kinds of communities they want. Ultimately, teacher communities must be judged in relationship to benefits or harms to students.

Communities have shifting borders that identify membership and beliefs. The cases demonstrated how communities negotiated and renegotiated such borders. The teachers formed an inclusive community when ties constructed bridges, rather than formed barriers, to those traditionally deemed outside of the community. Without a continued dialogue with multiple participants and perspectives, and an assumption of responsibility and care for students, parents, and other communities beyond the teachers, community building may result in harming "outsiders." A notion of inclusion and "an ethic of care" give rise to a "recognition of responsibility to one another" (Gilligan, 1982, pp. 28–30). While Washington's community teaches us about the power of caring ties among some teachers, it is in combination with an understanding of Chavez's more inclusive ties that we can conceive of a community that encompasses those teachers and students often marginalized and excluded from our schools.

Practitioners will want to engage in conversations about the inclusiveness of their community and their relationship to students and the broader local community. This will raise a number of questions. How do the borders they construct serve to build bridges, when appropriate? At what times might they want to identify strong boundaries of professionalism and delineate unacceptable beliefs or members? How could practitioners engage students, parents, and local community members in such a conversation about borders? What cultural, political, and professional divides might have to be bridged to hold this conversation?

CONCLUSION

Neither the antithesis of community nor aberrant behavior, conflict is central to community. Conflict is present at the inception of collaborative initiatives and continues throughout the communities' history as teachers expose divergent beliefs and practices. Although this idea is seemingly counterintuitive, conflict is a natural contributor to community. Rather than dismiss conflict as pathological or dysfunctional community behavior, these cases demonstrate how conflict is essential to some of the reform outcomes that community building in schools is supposed to produce. That is, conflict was linked to how a teacher community learned and changed over time. But, as the Chinese character symbolizes, both danger and opportunity may result from conflict. The way in which a teacher community approached these conflicts resulted in very different outcomes, costs, and benefits for teachers, communities, and schools.

While providing a strong sense of unity and satisfaction, a teacher community devoid of conflict was not as generative of reform as another more conflict-embracing one. Washington's teacher community may have successfully suppressed or transferred any differences and reaffirmed their strong bonds, but this actually limited their capacity to engage divergent thinking, new ideas, and an impetus for change. The end result, in the conflicts about students, undermined meeting the needs of up to 30% of their student population.

While often identified as fragmenting and stressful, a conflict-embracing community offered a potential for fostering ongoing organizational learning. Chavez teachers' more active engagement with professional conflicts opened up dialogue about differences in beliefs and practices that resulted in inquiry and change. This was particularly seen in their efforts to address the needs of their underserved African-American students. The debates over the IRISE initiative exposed divergent thinking, which pushed the faculty to explore their own capacity to reach students. This resulted in fostering significant changes.

Conflict ownership proved essential to organizational learning that involved deep inquiry and ongoing renewal. This kind of double-loop learning (Argyris & Schön, 1978) resulted when the faculty allowed their conflicts to challenge deeply held norms. When the teachers made space to disagree, to explain their differences, to listen to one another, to explore deeper dilemmas that lay beneath conflicts, and to experiment with alternative solutions, conflict proved critical to organizational learning.

Thus we must reframe the notion of conflict from the negative conception that abounds to a more hopeful one. Conflict represents a hopeful future for communities as they create a context for inquiry, growth, and change. A new view of conflict holds important implications for research, policy, and practice.

Researchers should expand their studies of community to incorporate an analysis of conflict and its relationship to organizational learning. Practitioners should consider enlarged professional roles for administrators and teachers as they engage in dialogue about differences. Policymakers and practitioners must provide systems and structures that support, rather than inhibit, productive conditions for conflict exploration. Practitioners should engage in conversations about how borders serve to bridge to or exclude the broader school community, especially students. For in the final analysis, how teacher communities serve students and schools is the measure of success.

How teacher communities define their own purpose, particularly as it relates to their ideology about schooling and students, proves vital in assessing what educational visions held by teacher communities are valuable in public schools. We must ask "community for what ends?" and evaluate which visions of schooling generated by teacher professional community are desirable for our schools.

To address the question of what educational visions we want teacher professional communities to have in our schools, I turn in the next chapter to explore ideologies of schooling promoted by each teacher professional community. Tied to each teacher community's ideology and stance toward conflict are visions about the purposes of schooling and its relationship to society. These ends are rarely examined or evaluated by researchers or practitioners.

NOTE

1. Personal communication with Anna Richert (1999) about the connection between inquiry and hope led to this thinking about conflict and hope.

CHAPTER 5

Beyond the Ties That Blind

In the previous chapter I shared the different kinds of learning and change that resulted from contrasting conflict stances. I addressed how one community learned in ways that promoted harmony and stability within the school while the other learned for the purpose of ongoing inquiry and change. In exploring the two teacher professional communities, I began to see the particular importance of their educational ideologies in shaping their conflict stances, and ultimately the kinds of learning and change that resulted in their schools. The communities I studied each held an ideology or framework of shared values about education, schooling, and students. The ideology included an orientation about student learning and outcomes, views about teachers' roles, notions about how schools should reform and change, and conceptions about the relationship between school and society. This ideology formed an educational vision through which teachers viewed their work, made sense of their world, and ultimately took action.

These educational visions are extremely important because they hold implications not only for teachers, but also for students, schools, and even society. For example, the teachers in one community viewed education as an institution of social change; thus their stance toward students was to create critical thinkers and change agents. Samuel, a Chavez teacher, compared this liberatory educational vision with a more conservative ideology that he saw enacted in most schools:

> [Others] want to educate students to maintain the status quo. . . .
> They want to teach them chemistry so they can do well in a chemistry class. But that person's never going to change the society. They'll go work for Dow Chemical. . . . I see what education should be as liberatory, it's to challenge the existing social system and change it.

How teacher communities envision influencing students and schooling should be the ultimate measure of what kinds of communities we want in our schools. Thus, in this final chapter I ask "community for what ends?" in order to answer the question *"What educational visions do we want teacher professional communities to have in our schools?"* I argue that given the current inequities found in both schools and society, a democratic communitarian vision that promotes greater social justice within and beyond the schoolhouse walls, balanced by a concern for stability and community, best meets the needs of public schools in our diverse American society.

VISIONS OF SCHOOLING IN TEACHER PROFESSIONAL COMMUNITIES

Teacher communities with vastly different visions of schooling are considered equally positive by some advocates, as long as these ideologies are shared within the community. But not all educational visions are equal. Different visions result in extremely different experiences for students, schools, broader educational communities, and society. Should we equally value educational visions that serve to bridge and those visions that form barriers between teachers and the larger school community? Should we prefer an educational ideology that challenges racial inequities in the service of social justice over one that tends to maintain the status quo in schools? Should we value conceptions that foster diversity over ones that sustain unity in our schools? These questions call for a deeper investigation into the visions of schooling promoted by teacher professional communities.

In exploring the conflict stances of two teacher professional communities, I began to see a spectrum of teacher community visions about schooling. One tends toward more democratic ends, aligned with goals of inclusion, participation, critique, and diversity. The other vision is more traditional, promoting harmony, stability, and reproduction of a common culture. Each vision holds both promises and dilemmas for teachers, schools, students, and society. Either vision, taken to an extreme, demonstrates the dark side of community. Too diverse and transforming a vision fosters disunity and instability (where diversity eclipses unity), while too traditional a notion promotes a type of conformity and intolerance (where unity suppresses diversity). Yet advocates of teacher professional communities may inadvertently be promoting only traditional visions, highlighting harmony and stability at the expense of diversity and transformation. I caution that these visions produce *ties that blind* communities to difference and conflict, and thus may undermine rich sources of growth and renewal for teachers, students, and schools.

This chapter explores a spectrum of teacher communities' educational visions in order to examine and evaluate these ends. Only through making these educational ideologies explicit can we begin to decide which ones are congruent with the goals of public schooling in American society. Ultimately, I argue for democratic communitarian visions for teacher professional communities, tempered by some of the strengths of more traditional goals. The democratic vision fosters space for access and participation, inquiry and critique of current conditions, and diversity of interests and participants— values necessary in publicly supported schools, which reflect our democratic society. These ends offer the potential for shaping a more socially just future. This vision, though, needs to be supported by some traditional values in order to sustain a wholeness that incorporates such diversity.

MODERN COMMUNITARIAN THOUGHT

To examine the visions promoted by teacher professional communities, I turn to communitarian writers concerned with the nature of relations in society. Educators often call on this literature to understand teacher community (see Sergiovanni, 1994; Westheimer, 1998), and in many ways, the cases I studied can be situated within a spectrum found within modern communitarian social thought.

Modern communitarian social theorists call for the development of stronger bonds and shared values in contrast to what they see as the fragmented and individualistic nature of American society (see Bellah et al., 1985; Etzioni, 1993; MacIntyre, 1981; Sandel, 1982). They are concerned with an atomistic vision of society as "constituted by individuals for the fulfillment of ends which were primarily individual" (Taylor, 1992, p. 29) and challenge an individualist liberal position, which focuses on the rights of individuals as autonomous entities to the detriment of communal responsibilities. Instead, they hope to supplant individualism by fostering enduring attachments and obligations, shared goals, and a sense of belonging within a bonded community. In this approach, they find the potential for creating a "good society" in common.

However, there is disagreement among modern communitarians about the nature of the good society. Within the group of modern communitarians, there are two distinct schools of thought, which can be called "traditional" and "democratic" (Kahne, 1996).

Traditional Communitarianism

Traditional communitarians advocate a shared conception of the good (harking back to Aristotle and Plato) as the basis for social harmony within society. They call for a common set of principles that bind individuals together and guide the moral well-being of society. In this approach, social harmony rather than conflict is at the core. Through the maintenance of traditional values and practices, individuals will find meaning and harmony as a collective. This approach highlights common agreements rooted in set traditional principles and values.

Amitai Etzioni (1993) proposes a traditional communitarian agenda to bring back into balance individual rights with responsibilities to the society. His hope lies in the preservation of strong traditional communities with their emphasis on shared values and morality. He calls for a return to a language of social virtues and obligations to one another. Etzioni places moral education in the hands of the community with its tools of suasion in making explicit the values that are acceptable and not acceptable in society. Communities, he finds, talk to us in moral voices. Alasdair MacIntyre (1981) concurs that "conceptions of good . . . can only be discovered by entering into those relationships which constitute communities whose central bond is a shared vision of and understanding of goods" (p. 240). Both Etzioni and MacIntyre rely on Aristotelian notions of fixed virtue, a common good understood by and agreed to by all and transcending any individual.

Democratic Communitarianism

Democratic communitarians criticize traditional communitarians for their static notion of community; restrictive roles and norms; limited diversity of perspectives; and lack of mechanisms for informed dissent, deliberation, and negotiation (Kahne, 1996). While democratic communitarians advocate the development of a shared life, appreciating the influence of community norms on individuals, they identify and embrace the diversity or broad range of interests and values held by individuals within a community. Rather than finding such diversity and the conflicts that arise from competing interests a threat to community, democratic communitarians see them as central to the development and growth of the community.

For example, John Dewey (1916) advocated for communities defined by informed dissent, constant growth, and flexible boundaries. Though I refer to it as democratic communitarianism, Dewey's philosophy also contains liberal and progressive perspectives. However, his work does provide an important contrast to both traditional communitarians and individualistic-oriented liberals. For him, the purpose of community was to foster communication and provide an environment for individual and collective inquiry and growth. Thus he emphasized the need for diversity within and interactions among communities.

John Dewey (1916) raised two questions to identify the strength of a community: (1) How numerous and varied are the interests that are consciously shared? and (2) How full and free is the interplay with other forms of association (p. 83)? Concerned with boundaries of groups, Dewey wrote, "The more numerous and varied points of contact devote a greater diversity of stimuli to which an individual has to respond . . . [in contrast to a] group which in its exclusiveness shuts out many interests" (p. 87). The future growth and development of communities, for Dewey, rested on criticism of the present. Thus dissenters, critics, and ultimately conflict played an essential role in growth. Dewey envisioned democratic communities as nonstatic, whereby future generations would criticize and improve on past generations.

EXAMINING TEACHER COMMUNITIES' EDUCATIONAL VISIONS

While modern communitarian theory addresses concerns of society at large, it also proves helpful in understanding educational ideologies. Teacher professional community advocates often refer to communitarian theory as a basis for the kinds of relations they hope to foster in schools. By drawing on parallels in communitarian theory, we see how teachers' notions about social relations apply to students, schools, and broader educational communities, and result in the enactment of very different kinds of schooling.

These two types of modern communitarian thought help to form a spectrum of visions held by teacher professional communities from *traditional* to *democratic* ends. The two cases I studied fall along this spectrum as hybrids (with both democratic and traditional visions), while tending toward different ends of the spectrum. To evaluate which visions we want for teacher communities, I will explore some of the critical issues that distinguish democratic from traditional goals, in particular highlighting the nature of participation, critique, and diversity held by each vision. These three issues make concrete how different educational ideologies held by teacher communities may shape the experience of teachers, schools, and students in the context of publicly supported schools within a diverse society.

Each vision offers both promises and dangers. One offers harmony, stability, and unity but risks conformity and at times intolerance. The other provides space for diversity and a transformative vision with the potential for disunity and instability. Given the current inequities within public schools and society today, I argue that a democratic vision with its potential for promoting greater social justice, tempered by some of the strengths of traditional values, aligns with the goals of publicly supported schools in a diverse and democratic society.

A Spectrum of Educational Visions

The democratic and traditional schools of communitarian thought help delineate a spectrum of educational visions held by teacher professional communities. These two points are situated on a much larger spectrum of educational ideologies, representing the variability of beliefs held by different teacher communities. A broader spectrum might include more radical notions held by critical theorists to the left of democratic visions, and liberal visions and conservative ideologies to the right. The traditional to democratic points represent a smaller spectrum of communitarian thought, within a larger continuum of diverse educational values. In between the traditional-democratic ends lie many hybrids that incorporate, to varying degrees, components of each end.

Traditional Communitarian Educational Visions. A traditional communitarian educational vision conceives of the role of schooling as one of socialization and reproduction, as a means to inculcate traditional values and shared conceptions of the good. Thus conflict is downplayed or seen as detrimental to achieving the valued ends of consensus around the common good.

Educational approaches aligned with this traditional communitarian vision call for schools to provide access to a common tradition. For example, Allan Bloom (1987) advocates for schools to foster a shared American heritage in order to construct a public good and E. D. Hirsch (1987) focuses on "cultural literacy" and decries the loss of common culture in our schools. Hirsch identifies the importance of schooling in generating a shared culture through the accumulation of common symbols and information. Some advocates of character education, such as Thomas Lickona (1997), would similarly align with a traditional communitarian vision in calling for a "recovery of shared, objectively important ethical values . . . such values as respect, responsibility, trustworthiness, fairness, caring, and civil virtue" (p. 55). By restoring a traditional morality shared by all, such advocates hope to promote the good of individuals and the collective.

In an extreme and problematic example of a traditional communitarian vision, Alan Peshkin portrays teachers at the Bethany Baptist Academy (a private fundamentalist Christian school) in *God's Choice* (1986). The teacher community shares a common tradition as expressed in Scripture. Peshkin portrays both the powerful feelings of unity and belonging in such a community of the "saved" and the clear boundaries drawn around such a community, which rejects nonbelievers and values outside of the orthodoxy. Peshkin is thus able to shed light on the darker side of the kind of community that is fostered by these teachers. Drawing on Goffman (1961), Peshkin identifies the community as a "total institution," one that controls the entire life of the individuals involved and allows no deviance from traditional church values. Ultimately, he concludes that such a setting is unacceptable given the context of our diverse democratic society.

Democratic Communitarian Educational Visions. In contrast, the democratic communitarian vision finds school a site for critiquing and reforming society. Educational approaches aligned with this democratic communitarian vision call for schools to provide opportunities for social connection, participation, inquiry, access to multiple perspectives, and respect for diversity. This vision also entails seeing schools as breeding grounds for critique and transformation through critical questioning and a social-justice focus (Darling-Hammond, 1997; Dewey, 1916; Giroux, 1988; Gutman, 1987). Here, conflict is core to the practices of transformation and change.

John Dewey (1916) epitomizes this democratic communitarian educational vision. He believed that schooling was the best way to foster a sense of democratic community in the next generation and to provide fertile ground for improving and transforming both individuals and the outside community. Schools could be nurseries for democratic community. This meant not just teaching about the institutions of government, but participating in a mini-society that practiced the principles of democratic community. Dewey's version of schooling as a democratic community was a transformative model that "endeavor[s] to shape the experience of the young so that instead of reproducing current habits, better habits shall be formed, and thus the future adult society can be an improvement on their own" (p. 79).

The democratic vision could also include more reform-oriented democratic theorists—advocates of teaching for social action such as William Ayers (1993) and others, such as Henry Giroux (1983), who write about the role of resistance, critical theory, and struggle for social democracy in education. Giroux calls for a radical pedagogy that involves educators' linking critique to social transformation. "Radical pedagogy needs to be informed by a passionate faith in the necessity of struggling to create a better world," writes Giroux; "in other words, radical pedagogy needs a vision—one that celebrates not what is but what could be" (p. 242).

In between these two communitarian ends lie hybrids that represent a mixture of traditional and democratic communitarian educational purposes. For instance, there are versions of teachers' ideologies that promote schooling for civic values (e.g., participation in voting and service to the community), stopping short of the more critical or social-justice mission of more reform-oriented democratic ends.

Washington and Chavez Teacher Communities' Visions. While each tended toward different ends of the spectrum, the teacher professional communities I studied reflect two hybrids along the spectrum of communitarian thought. The Washington teacher community's vision of schooling and society was closer to traditional communitarianism in its emphasis on unanimity of beliefs, low dissent, and norms to conserve the status quo and minimize questioning the values of the community.

The traditional communitarian vision downplays the role of conflict, diversity, and critical dialogue about collective values of the group. In this same way, Washington teachers avoided or transferred conflict, thus conserving the unity and traditions of the group, ultimately promoting stability. Washington teachers acknowledged that their vision was, as one teacher reported, "not about changing society." Their vision statement included language about promoting students to become "productive and responsible members" of the community and to give service to it, thus inculcating students with a sense of responsibility within given social relations.

In contrast, Chavez exhibited more democratic tendencies by embracing diversity, dissent, and practices to foster change. Chavez teachers put conflict at the center of their work, criticizing the status-quo system of schooling. Like that of democratic communitarians, Chavez's vision of schooling and society allowed for a broad range of interests to play out in the school and a free interplay between the multiple stakeholders within and beyond the school.

Chavez teachers did not want to reproduce the inequality that exists in the larger society. They had a vision that school can reduce inequity and serve to reform society. The teachers envisioned themselves as agents of social change. Their consent-decree status put their democratic principles at the forefront of their work and in the front hallway of their building: "All children should learn to live and work in a world that is characterized by interdependence and cultural diversity. All individuals are entitled to be treated with respect and dignity." Ultimately, Chavez's vision aligns more closely with the democratic communitarian one, which promotes an inclusive, critical, and diverse community.

Each community's conflict stance was crucial in exposing and shaping these larger purposes. One community sought to avoid conflict in order to sustain tradition, harmony, and stability within the current schooling system, ultimately serving to socialize students into the values held in larger society. The other, at times, solicited and embraced conflict as a way to critique the system, hoping to transform relations within the larger society.

From Traditional to Democratic Visions:
Examining Critical Differences

To illustrate the spectrum of visions and to evaluate preferred ends, I turn to examine critical issues of how teacher communities' educational visions may differ around conceptions of participation, critique, and diversity. I highlight these three issues because the case studies exposed differences that reflect significant variations along the spectrum and because participation, critique, and diversity impact the experience of teachers, schools, and students within the context of publicly supported schools in our democratic society.

Participation: From Exclusive to Inclusive Communities. Communities are characterized by their levels of participation (Selznick, 1992). Participation defines the amount of active engagement in community life. It also refers to borders that delineate which members and what beliefs are considered part of the community. While a traditional vision offers a sense of belonging by delineating insider status, a democratic vision is more inclusive, building bridges to those beyond the community in ways that expand membership and beliefs. While both visions have much to offer, the traditional vision taken to an extreme erects barriers that ultimately reduce interaction with the broader school community. A democratic vision that promotes inclusivity, still tempered by a traditional sense of belonging and care, may best meet the needs of teacher communities, students, and schools.

Traditional communitarian educational visions foreground notions of belonging and commitment that result from membership. Such a community constructs a strong and recognizable group identity of those within and outside. For teachers, this is particularly appealing given the experience of isolation and uncertainty in their own classrooms (Little, 1990a; Lortie, 1975). Fostering caring relationships, moral support, help, and friendship among those who belong in the community is also an appealing image (Noddings, 1992). A sense of belonging, connectedness, and obligation to one another is a powerful antidote to the alienation experienced in most public schools. For example, the "loving, warm, and extremely close collaboration" that a Washington teacher described enabled the faculty to develop an ethic of care for one another inside of their community. In most school settings, fostering a sense of caring between teachers is a challenge because of their isolation in their own classrooms, and their norms of autonomy and individualism (Noddings, 1992). Washington's stance toward conflict, one sensitive to relationships and bonds of community, served an important function for teachers.

Identifying strong borders of membership of a community also serves to increase the professional identity of teachers. Noneducators feel all too comfortable pronouncing what should be done in schools. Teachers have long struggled to be perceived as professionals. Professionals share a common knowledge base, control entry and conditions of work, and most importantly determine the agreed-on technical knowledge that is central to their field (Louis & Kruse, 1995). Identifying an exclusive community of professionals serves to highlight the specialized status of teachers. When the local teacher community determines shared values and common beliefs, it offers schools a sense of mission and focus as is particularly seen in private, religious, charter, or magnet schools (Bryk, Lee, & Holland, 1983).

Yet the root word *munio* found in the Latin *communis* (community) means "to provide with defensive fortifications" (Glare, 1990, cited in Calderwood, 2000, p. 6). This same movement to define a sense of belonging and identity constructs borders that define outsider status. Such borders delineating membership and beliefs can form barriers or bridges to others. While borders are central to the creation of group identity, the permeability of a community's borders—how exclusive or inclusive it is—holds implications for schooling.

At Washington, as the walls grew high around the professional community they served to isolate teachers from students, parents, and the neighborhood. Washington's construction of "others," those deemed outsiders, built barriers to certain students and parents, with disturbing results. A conflict about students promoted blaming students and their parents, leaving unexamined teachers' own practice and allowing teachers to relinquish responsibility for a portion of their student population. Such a stance transfers away individual and collective agency, disempowering professionals by limiting the conception of their sphere of influence.

Drawing such tightly constructed and impermeable borders around a community also has implications for issues of social justice—who is written into your community and who is written out. Ginsberg (1994) argues that the farther removed one is from "others," the greater the loss of responsibility to them (cited in Calderwood, 2000, p. 14). Similarly, Noddings (1989; 1996) warns that one of the dangers of border negotiation is that when a community draws a circle around itself, erects barriers, and puts the other outside of the moral community, otherness is identified as something to be converted or assimilated.

What happens if some students are perceived of as outside the moral community? At Washington, "problem" students, parents, and teachers were deemed outside the community. They were labeled "nonparticipants" in community life, and ultimately marginalized or expelled. This resulted in the exclusion of up to 30% of the student population.

Little and McLaughlin (1993) found that "collegial interactions or notions of a good colleague in some settings may conceivably diverge from what is good for children, what is good practice, or what is good for the education enterprise more generally" (p. 5). Hammersley (1984) and Woods (1984) similarly found staffroom interactions that supported solidarity among teachers through the use of humor at the expense of their students. Thus, insulting students became acceptable and even encouraged behavior within the teacher community. Ultimately, as Little (1990b) explains, "the relations that teachers establish with fellow teachers or with other adults will—and must—be judged by their ability to make teachers' relations with students more productive and more satisfying" (p. 167). Teacher communities should be judged by their responsiveness to and inclusiveness of *all* students. This raises dilemmas for teacher communities when connections to colleagues and those to students conflict. Such was the case at Washington. When one teacher questioned the practice of suspending students perceived to be "problematic," a colleague responded, "Aren't we going to support our own [teachers]?"

A democratic vision is more inclusive, fostering open borders that form bridges to those beyond the community, ultimately expanding membership and beliefs. The "full and free interplay with other forms of association" was central to Dewey's conception of community (1916, p. 83). As Gardner states, "The traditional community was often unwelcoming to strangers, and all too ready to reduce its communication with the external world" (1991, p. 11). Values that foster inclusivity have much to offer teachers and schools.

At Chavez, the teacher community often identified with students and parents, fostering permeable borders, and ultimately bringing the students and parents into the teachers' realm of responsibility. Teachers confronted one another about the needs of students of color in their school, realizing that, as one Chavez teacher explained, "we are sending too many African-American boys to the counseling office." In this way, conflict served to build bridges to students, rather than barriers. Such an inclusive community expands the moral responsibility and capacity of teachers. Smiley (1992) describes how a community's boundaries shape the presence or absence of conceptions of moral responsibility and social justice. If the borders of care include the other, one's own status can impel one to eradicate injustices experienced by the other person or group. Such inclusive borders are vital in a service profession like teaching, where adults have responsibility for *all* children. Professional commitment is thus tied to students in an inclusive community, expanding the realm of responsibility and care.

Teacher communities are situated within an environment that includes multiple communities, including students, but also parents and neighborhoods. These communities beyond the teachers' community provide feedback, critique, and new ways of thinking that could foster growth. Recent research has begun to address the relationship between schools and their external community (parents, neighborhood, etc.), identifying the importance of public engagement and empowerment in schools (see Lutz & Merz, 1992). Strengthening the linkages among schools, parents, and communities through school-based management, parent involvement, and coordinated services is seen as a mechanism to improve educational outcomes for students (Merz & Furman, 1997; Purkey & Smith, 1983). For example, Chavez staff actively engaged parents in the governance bodies of the school, making decisions about program, curriculum, and policy. A parent advocate was employed to increase community involvement in the school. An evening discussion group engaged parents, students, and teachers in monthly dialogue about equity and schooling. Student-facilitated "portfolio conversations" for parents replaced traditional parent-teacher conferences. Chavez, with its open borders, became potentially more responsive to its communities, solicited the voices of stakeholders in decision-making, and worked collaboratively with partners to develop a coordinated effort to improve the lives of students.

Teacher communities that foster democratic purposes provide a potential for inclusion of ever broader communities, building bridges to rather than barriers between teachers, students, and parents. Such broad participation needs some balancing, though, with traditional values, in order to define membership and a sense of belonging within the professional community. Otherwise, borders become permeable to the point of invisibility, leaving no sense of community at all.

Critique: From Mainstream to Critical Communities. Schools provide both a site of socialization into the values held by our society and a fertile ground for potentially transforming society. In a democratic society education plays a key role in acculturating the next generation to actively participate in society and also promotes the development of critical thinkers who can serve to improve society. Therefore, both mainstream and critical schooling ends are essential to teacher communities. Yet, given the current state of schooling in America with its widening achievement gap, a mainstream approach that sustains current conditions left unbalanced by critique does not bode well for many students, particularly poor ones and students of color. In contrast, a vision that challenges current practices and the reproduction of inequality in schooling, tempered with some socializing forces, offers greater promise in promoting equality in society.

The traditional vision promotes the maintenance of values and practices that foster harmony and congruence with the past. Bellah et al. (1985) write about how communities have a history, that they are "constituted by their past." They advocate for "communities of memory" that do not forget their past (p. 153). School and teacher communities that align with such a vision promise congruence and harmony with the society, offering stronger mechanisms for socialization of the next generation into the very values that make up a "good society." Building on traditions is important in maintaining a common culture within the community.

This vision of community is in harmony with the outside environment and dominant messages from beyond the schoolhouse walls. Schools, as public institutions, must be somewhat responsive to and reflective of the dominant political climate of their local community and the larger society. Washington's tendencies to uphold mainstream conceptions of education, identifying schools as sites for socialization into the current system, promote such a vision. The congruence between Washington teachers' ideology of schooling and the larger society's expectations for schooling elicited less conflict and functioned as a stabilizing influence.

Most teacher communities are fragile. Teachers move from one school to another, in and out of the profession, and do not often develop a tradition. Furthermore, unlike the professions of medicine and law, a core knowledge base or technology of teaching is still quite contested, leading to a lack of a common set of teacher customs. Certain schools (particularly private schools with long-standing histories) offer an interesting case of strong communities of tradition, with shared rituals and customs. The particular focus on documenting school history and knowing those who have come before, is a powerful drive toward a community of memory.

The traditional vision downplays the role of conflict, diversity, and critical dialogue about the collective values of the group. Such a community conserves the traditions of the group, promotes stability, and minimizes a need for questioning shared values (Kahne, 1996). For teacher communities, conflict avoidance and maintenance of traditions can serve to stabilize schools, sustain coordination, and promote teacher retention.

The benefits of a mainstream-identified community should not be underestimated in a time of reform hyperactivity (Fullan, 1993) or chaotic school change. Washington's case exhibited these benefits offered by the traditional communitarian vision. Washington teachers sustained stability, preserved traditions, and retained teachers over time, while Chavez teachers experienced the frenetic pace of change and confusion, at times resulting in stress and turnover. Such turnover of teachers may have negatively impacted students. When I shared information on this study about the practices at Chavez, Washington teachers were in agreement that they would never be able to work at a school as conflictual and chaotic as Chavez.

Some organizational theorists find "embracing conflicts" attractive, glorifying moments of chaos or "organized anarchy" as "creative" (Bolman & Deal, 1984; Cohen, March, & Olsen, 1976; Fullan, 1993). But what is the toll that this takes? An ongoing process of deep questioning resulting in fundamental organizational change is taxing. Exhaustion from challenging, deconstructing, and then inventing everything from the ground up means that routinization rarely occurs and teacher time is enormously taxed by generating and learning new things. Such ambiguity was less palatable to those subjected to anarchical circumstances—teachers trying to make safe and supportive climates for themselves and their students who had already experienced enough chaos in their lives. Hargreaves (1997) objects that these theorists seem to "revel in contradictions." "Reinvented as paradoxes, chaos and complexity, these deeply painful contradictions for practitioners have become symbolic tokens of hope and exhortation in what is often an academic ecstasy of change theory and change advocacy" (p. 3).

Students may suffer from a sense of instability as well. As teacher turnover occurs, divisions between faculty members and subsequent differentiation of teaching practices that result from less unified staff may diminish students' educative experiences.

While potentially more chaotic, the democratic vision that embraces conflict allows for challenges and critique of the current society, such that improvements can be made. This more critical vision identifies schools as sites of challenge to society. Such was the case with Chavez's community, which placed critique of society and current systems of schooling at the core. Chavez's more critical ideology, which defined schools as sites for transformation and social justice, challenged the status quo found in society. In trying to invent a counterculture, the community found itself in conflict with dominant ideologies in the broader environment. This clash was further accentuated by the lack of prevailing models in the environment from which the community could draw. Thus conflict was generated as teachers argued about competing approaches to "the good school" and "the good society."

Schooling can provide grounds for renewing society. Teacher professional communities that uphold these democratic visions of schooling challenge prevailing practices that reproduce inequalities in our schools and ultimately in society. They promote a vision of social justice and change through their ideology of critique and practices of dissent. Such a vision allows for changes toward more just schools and society. Again, this critical vision must be tempered by some traditional values, which reduce the sense of chaos and instability that critical visions, when taken to an extreme, may produce. A vision that continually deconstructs society, without space for reconstruction and reproduction of preferred values, is destabilizing for both students and teachers.

Diversity: From Bonded to Diverse Communities. There is much to be said for teacher communities that promote a vision of unity, but this same vision can undermine the goal of fostering diversity within community in our public schools.

The traditional vision offers a unified picture reminiscent of small-town life, where homogeneity and common ties outweighed differences. A sense of "we-ness" surpassed subgroup or individual diversity. The bond served to foster ties of obligation and responsibility to one another, a sense of belonging and identity, and a potential to collectively construct a good society. This vision has much to offer both teachers and schools.

Current research on teacher communities applauds bonded or socially cohesive communities such as Washington's. Here, members all work collaboratively with a high degree of commitment toward common goals. Bonded communities are remarkable for their level of consensus and unanimity. Teachers suffer from individualism, alienation, and isolation within their work cultures (Hargreaves, 1994; Little, 1990a; Lortie, 1975; Rosenholtz, 1989). Envisioning bonded communities counters this negative culture. Similarly, Nias, Southworth, and Yeomans (1989) found that a strong culture of collaboration leads to greater consensus and a sense of collective strength, interdependence, and mutual security.

Bonded teacher communities also seek to counter the norms of fragmentation or balkanization often found in secondary schools. A balkanized teacher community, warns Hargreaves (1992), results when teachers' identity and loyalty are attached to particular groups within a school and reinforce differential beliefs and practices. Balkanization may result in poor coordination within schools, lack of continuity for students, and territorial conflicts; limit opportunities for exchange and change at schoolwide level; and contribute to a sense of alienation within schools (Hargreaves, 1994).

At times Chavez's teacher community came close to such balkanization and fragmentation because of its stance toward difference and conflict. During the IRISE debates, teachers exposed deep divisions about beliefs and practices in regard to teaching African-American students. There were dramatic disagreements about segregation and desegregation. Only two teachers would be initiating the IRISE program, and they would be pulling African-American students out of the diverse student setting. At other times, the strong individualism and subgroup identities overtook their communal ones. Such was the case with an eighth-grade teacher who challenged his team. One could envision this lack of coordination among teachers as negatively impacting the students as they experienced inconsistencies in practice. Moreover, consensus and unity were often quite fragile at Chavez.

The nature of their personal and professional ties, and the homogeneity of their teacher population and beliefs, served to foster a bonded community at Washington Middle School. Such ties resulted at times in powerful collaboration among teachers, fulfilling the promise of reform advocates interested in tight coordination of practice across a school. Washington teachers were engaged in collective curriculum design and were found to be teaching the same kinds of lessons from classroom to classroom. Their friendship served as a source of deep connection and common ground for doing collective work. Their students experienced a consistency of practice as their teachers acted in unison, reinforcing each other's strategies and teachings.

And yet, this vision of bonding is also problematic for teacher professional communities and schools. The relational metaphors of friendship and family should be highly suspect in teachers' work culture, which is constrained by political and professional obligations as well. Friendship at work creates unique dilemmas for teachers. A key dimension of friendship, acceptance of friends as they are, counters critical professional judgment of coworkers (Bridge & Baxter, 1992). Friends are less likely to challenge one another's behaviors. At Washington such ties were, as one teacher explained, "worse for conflict, because it's personal; it's your friends" and resulted in conflict avoidance since confrontation would rupture personal and professional relationships. Lima (1998) found that some interpersonal ties in schools limited or destroyed teachers' opportunities for professional development and growth as friends reduced access to alternative perspectives on how to meet students' needs and did not address improper professional conduct. Such was the case at Washington. This impacted students negatively, as teachers limited opportunities to examine practices that failed to reach a possible 30% of their students.

Similarly, romanticizing conceptions of family in schools ignores inequality of status and power, as well as the dysfunctional nature of many family units. As feminists warn, such traditional settings are often oppressive contexts for individuality or minority perspectives (Millet, 1970). While Washington teachers identified as a family, they clearly labeled and treated differently the stepchildren and the black sheep.

The traditional notion of a bonded community is most unsettling when conceived of as a homogeneous one undermining the diversity that makes up the context of modern society and public schools. Alternatively, the democratic communitarian vision offers a conception that reflects the diversity of our American schools and society. Teachers and students from diverse racial, ethnic, linguistic, religious, cultural, and class backgrounds are required to join together. More generally, a democratic vision holds that publicly supported schools are settings in which students learn about our society and develop tolerance for diversity, as well as learn about their commonalities as Americans. Though we share a common culture, one aspect of our commonness is our diversity, our respect for disagreement, and our individual and subgroup affiliations.

Washington teachers' unanimity of beliefs, avoidance of conflict, and bonded ties highlighted commonality. In contrast, Chavez teachers supported the diversity in their midst, from individual dissent to strong subgroup affiliations, to overt conflicts over teachers' beliefs and practices, to critical debate about race and student needs. While they sought commonalities especially with their shared ideology, they also recognized the importance of a diversity of interests, identities, and affiliations.

Education is central to the promise of democracy. In a political and economic sense, students are schooled to participate in future civic and work arenas. But education also provides a vehicle for creating social participation (Darling-Hammond, 1997). Children learn how to be in community with a diverse population. Such a democratic vision of community in schools fosters diversity within unity. Why this unity in diversity asks Philip Selznick. "The answer lies in what it means to share a *common* life. A common life is not a *fused* life" (1992, p. 369).

This study challenges us to transform the current dichotomization of unity and diversity. It is a false dichotomy that places them in opposition or imagines that one cancels the other out. Given the reality of our multicultural society, we can no longer afford to be nostalgic about a homogeneous past. Neither fusion nor complete individuation is the answer. Rather, communities must include individualism, group affiliation, diverse cultures and beliefs, along with a framework of shared purposes. Iris Marion Young (1990) posits a "politics of difference" within communities that embraces a form of cultural pluralism, which does not eliminate or transcend group differences. Young finds that "there is equality among socially and culturally differentiated groups, who mutually respond to one another and affirm one another in their differences" (p. 163). In this way difference is not something to be excluded, opposed, or dominated.

Similarly, John Gardner (1991) describes "wholeness incorporating diversity" as the transcendent goal of our time. Gardner explains:

> Diversity is not simply "good" in that it implies breadth of tolerance and sympathy. A community of diverse elements has greater capacity to adapt and renew itself in a swiftly changing world. But to speak of community implies some degree of wholeness. What we seek—at every level—is pluralism that achieves some kind of coherence, *wholeness incorporating diversity.* (p. 15)

Gardner's notion celebrates diversity within wholeness for the sake of a process of renewal and change within the community. He is careful to point out that wholeness incorporating diversity involves a careful balancing act. To keep the wholeness from smothering diversity, Gardner advocates an openness to dissent and an opportunity for subcommunities to maintain their identity and be active in developing whole-group goals. To keep diversity from destroying wholeness, he identifies the need for structures to reduce polarization, to foster communication between diverse groups, and mechanisms for conflict mediation. It is thus through a vision of wholeness incorporating diversity that teacher professional communities may best serve students, schools, and ultimately society.

BEYOND THE TIES THAT BLIND

The issues addressed above of participation, critique, and diversity demonstrate how teacher communities' ideologies contain very different visions of schooling that span from more traditional to more democratic communitarian ends. I return now to the question that I began with: What educational visions do we want teacher professional communities to have in our schools? If we want to promote more unity and stability, then teacher communities that produce more traditional values are the way to go. If we want to support goals of inclusion, critique, and diversity, then I argue that teacher communities that support democratic ends have the greater potential to get us there.

While there are genuine benefits to both ends of the communitarian spectrum, one side of the spectrum is more consistent with the goals of public schooling within a democratic society. One side tries to improve on current relations found in society and promotes the kinds of participation, dissent, and commitment to a discourse on difference needed in a democratic society. The teacher communities that serve democratic ends align more with stated goals for public education in America.

The answer to which vision of community is desirable is still not that simple, however. Many challenges remain. While democratic ends are necessary, so too are some traditional values. For instance, there needs to be a certain level of wholeness, a unity of purpose within which a diversity of perspectives and practices can still emerge. It takes both dissent and consensus for communities to move forward. Ultimately, it will take a careful mixture of democratic and traditional teacher community values to benefit both schools and society.

The teacher professional community literature in many ways overly emphasizes a traditional communitarian vision, especially in approaches to conflict and diversity. This study of two professional communities has exposed the necessity to reexamine and challenge the reform rhetoric that finds overly traditional communities resilient and strong. In light of these insights, we must reconsider the *binding* nature of such communities. Whereas advocates of this vision call for binding as a way for professionals to commit to a set of shared values and ideas (Sergiovanni, 1994), I have found that these same ties that bind can serve as the ties that blind us from understanding the differences, conflicts, and diversity found within communities. Alternatively, we have seen some of the hazards raised by a loss of the connections that tie communities together.

We need to explore a multiplicity of ties beyond those that blind or those that totally fragment a community. This means examining the strength of weak ties (Granovetter, 1973) or less intimate and developed relationships. Iris Marion Young (1995) moves away from the term *community* altogether, concerned about its fused quality, and calls instead for social relationships with an "openness to unassimilated otherness" (p. 253). Gardner's (1991) "wholeness incorporating diversity" is central to a new understanding of community. "The play of conflicting interests in a framework of shared purposes" is the image needed for our schools and society (p. 15). The challenge then is how to conceptualize a community that maintains the ties and connectedness of a caring and stable community while sustaining the diversity, critical perspectives, and inclusiveness of an ongoing learning community.

Examining, rather than overlooking, the role of conflict amid community is critical to this endeavor. Conflict generates opportunities to strengthen communities, for in the conflict lies an occasion to examine differences of beliefs, solicit alternative voices, bridge across differences, and seek opportunities for change and growth.

In sum, the educational visions of teacher professional communities hold enormous implications for students, schools, and even society. The two cases helped reveal different kinds of educational ideologies and their effects on schooling. In the translation of communitarian theory into practice within schools, these distinguishing visions matter deeply in how teachers act and how students experience schooling. I have found that educational visions that highlight values of inclusion, critique, and diversity, balanced by some traditional communitarian notions, may best meet the needs of our schools. But it is a careful balancing act to sustain wholeness incorporating diversity, to maintain differences of belief and practice while sustaining unity. It is something to be continually negotiated and renegotiated by teachers, their professional community, and the broader educational community.

A FINAL REFLECTION

I often think about my experiences in Chicago as part of the school reform movement and as a founding member of a school interested in fostering a democratic community among teachers and students. I also puzzle about the challenges we faced. I remember most my silence when Brooke, the only African-American teacher on my team, announced that she wanted all of the African-American girls in her advisory group because she felt they needed her and that they would not listen to the rest of us.

In my mind I like to replay that conversation with my teacher team at Thurgood Marshall Middle School. I have no illusions that it would be an easy conversation, if we had had one. As Gardner (1991) said, "The play of conflicting interests in a framework of shared purposes is the drama of a free society. It is a robust exercise and a noisy one, not for the fainthearted or the tidy-minded" (p. 15).

I think about my anger, guilt, and pain. I also think about the challenging questions I should have asked, the passionate statements of beliefs that should have been shared, and the conflicts that would have been exposed. As a result of Brooke's challenge to my philosophy, my own approach to teaching might have changed. Brooke's views might have shifted. The students' experience would certainly have been different.

I know this dialogue would have both challenged our cohesion and strengthened our community. We would have had to give language to differences of professional beliefs about race, equity, and schooling. It would have pushed us to consider and reconsider teaching, schooling, and ourselves.

I know I will not stay silent at such an opportunity again.

Methodological Appendix

This methodological appendix addresses further details about data collection and analysis used in this study.

DATA COLLECTION

Data collection involved four major sources: interviews, observation, documents, and a survey. I describe each below.

Interviews

I conducted tape-recorded semi-structured interviews with 44 key teachers, administrators, and other school personnel from two informant populations: participating teachers and administrators and a subgroup of eighth-grade target teachers, who were involved more intensively. Participating teachers and administrators (16 individuals from each school) were selected via "snowball sampling" whereby key informants were referred through other informants based on their perspective or participation in conflicts. I approached key informants based on these recommendations and gave them the option to participate. I tried to select teachers who might bring different perspectives, including male and female, new and experienced, as well as teachers of different races and ethnicities, and from different subjects/grade levels.

I conducted interviews early on in the study to explore issues of teacher community, specifically whether teachers felt a sense of community, how they defined community, and how the community dealt with differences and conflicts. I used a hypothetical scenario of two schools that handled a specific conflict differently as an eliciting device. I then asked if there were conflicts of this kind or others at their school. I also asked about the outcomes of such conflicts in terms of the teacher community.

Next, I chose a subgroup of target teachers within each school (seven at Chavez; five at Washington), who comprised a grade-level team (eighth grade), with which to conduct a more intensive series of interviews. This concentrated study provided a "case within a case" that added another layer of depth to the schoolwide study. With this group I conducted initial interviews similar to those with participating teachers, adding some questions about their team experience. I also conducted a series of follow-up individual interviews with the target teachers to reflect on their earlier interviews and any new issues of conflict that had arisen. These teachers were interviewed from two to five times during the study.

A sample of the interview questions includes:

1. How would you describe how teachers work together at your school?

2. Let's turn to issues of difference, controversy, or conflict in teacher professional communities. My research interest relates to the question how teacher professional communities approach or respond to conflicts. Let me give you two stories and then ask you some questions about whether you have any experiences like or unlike these at your school.

In one teacher professional community, the faculty discussed adopting a multicultural curriculum throughout the school to better reflect their diverse student population. In meeting to discuss these ideas, conflicts arose over what and how to teach specific subjects and the underlying meaning of multiculturalism in education. This in turn touched deeper racial struggles experienced by faculty in the school. Teachers began to confront each other about racial differences. This school began to provide open discussion and debate about these issues that enabled the teacher professional community to face some hard questions and realize deep conflicts without polarizing the school. Teachers decided they needed to be more comfortable discussing these difficult issues of racial conflict if they expected their students to do the same. Some outcomes of these discussions included a revamped curriculum with a more integrated approach to multiculturalism in all disciplines and continued forums for discussion on issues of race. The teachers had embraced the conflict as a source of learning and change for the school. They also became a community more open to discussing issues of difference and more sensitive to racial conflicts in their school.

In another teacher professional community, teachers were deciding whether to join a new reform initiative that would involve more teacher collaboration on teams and time spent on shared school decision-making. A small group of younger faculty received money from the principal to write a proposal for the reform. The proposal went to the full faculty and passed by a slim margin. As teachers began to meet in planning teams, conflicts arose over whether teachers should spend time collaborating and making school governance decisions or spend time in the classroom. They also experienced conflicts over who got power and money within the school. These conflicts resulted in splitting the faculty. Some teachers were labeled "resisters." They felt resentful about not being listened to and for being negatively labeled for their cautions against reforms that took attention away from the classroom. Those advocates of the reform saw the "resisters" as traditional teachers unwilling to change. The reform efforts were ultimately blocked as the teacher professional community became polarized by the conflict. Teacher relations were strained by the conflict making communication across the two polarized groups extremely difficult.

2a. What issues of difference or conflicts have arisen between teachers at your school? Has there been any controversy, struggle, or conflict between teachers like these described in the stories or of another kind?

2b. Can you think of two or three events that represent how your staff deals with differences or conflicts among teachers? Can you tell me about them?

3. What techniques of managing, negotiating, or thinking about conflict has this community offered? What is the communities' stance toward conflicts?

5. What was the outcome of those conflicts? How did they impact the teacher community?

6. How does the staff deal with those who disagree with decisions that a majority of the staff endorses? Can you think of a time that happened? Can you tell me about it?

Observation

I was able to observe teachers for over 4 years (intensively examining issues of conflict over 2 years) at one school, and 1 year at the second site. I observed 1 to 4 days a week at each site over the course of the study. I took extensive fieldnotes, audiotaped formal meetings, and wrote memos and vignettes from significant observations. I observed both formal and informal meetings. Examples of formal meetings included governance council, department, grade-level, whole-school, teamed teachers, professional development, and various committees. These gatherings offered access to interactions between and among teachers where conflicts often emerged, and were sometimes discussed and managed. Observations of these teacher interactions offered a source of information beyond self-reporting (i.e., surveys and interviews) that aided in triangulation. Informal settings were also observed, including the teacher's lounge, main office, copy room, and extracurricular events.

I also observed a subgroup (eighth-grade-level team) target population on an ongoing basis. With this group, I observed more regularly interactions in formal and informal settings, such as team planning meetings, social gatherings, and the like.

Documents

I collected a variety of documents, including minutes from meetings, school portfolios, School Report Cards, policy documents, internal memos, and historical artifacts and texts. The goal was to place the current teacher conflicts in historical context and to trace any patterns of approaches to and outcomes of conflict. These materials were another source for triangulation.

Survey

I adapted a survey from McLaughlin and Talbert (1996), and distributed it to the whole faculty at each school. Of the 61 respondents, 28 or 97% of Washington's certified staff participated, and 33 or 79% of Chavez's certified staff participated. The survey drew from my conceptual framework and addressed the sources of, and approaches to, conflict within teacher commuities. This survey included questions regarding teacher demographics, norms of teacher community, beliefs about and understandings of conflict, and teachers' work culture. This schoolwide data source provided more comprehensive information about the schools and their approaches to conflict. The survey findings both challenged and confirmed my emerging theories. Exploratory factor analysis of the survey was used to identify a number of key constructs described in this study. A sample of the individual survey items that formed some of the key concepts follows. Several survey items made up each factor. The letters reflect the actual survey item (e.g., items a, b, c, e, g, n, o, and p formed a factor identified as "teacher learning community").

Teacher-learning-community Measures. Please indicate the extent to which you agree or disagree with each of the following statements about professional relations in your school. (Scale 1–5) (Factor loading of at least .62)

a. There is a great deal of cooperative effort among the staff members.
b. Teachers in this school are continually learning and seeking new ideas from each other.
c. Teachers in this school keep to themselves. (reverse coded)
e. Teachers critically reflect together about the challenges and successes of the school.
g. Teachers in this school identify themselves as being part of a whole-school community.
n. Teachers regularly meet to discuss particular common problems and challenges we are facing in the classroom.
o. Teachers share beliefs and values about what the central mission of the school should be.
p. Teachers in this school believe all students can succeed.

Embrace-conflict Measures. Please indicate the extent to which you agree or disagree with each of the following statements about how teachers at your school respond to conflict. (Scale 1–5) (Factor loadings of .61 or above)

    a. Teachers in this school acknowledge differences and conflict as a natural part of school life.
    c. The staff seldom evaluates its programs and activities. (reverse coded)
    e. Our stance toward our work is one of inquiry and reflection.
    f. Teachers are open to perspectives different from their own.
    g. Teachers at this school understand that conflict is inevitable when they collaborate.
    o. Teachers here see differences and conflict as an opportunity for learning.

Avoid-conflict Measures. Please indicate the extent to which you agree or disagree with each of the following statements about how teachers at your school respond to conflict. (Scale 1–5) (Factor loadings of .66 or above)

    b. We tend to avoid conflicts between teachers.
    h. When conflict arises between teachers we usually "sweep it under the rug."
    i. After a conflict, we quickly try to reunite as a faculty. (reverse coded)

Stress Measures. Please indicate the extent to which you agree or disagree with each of the following statements about how teachers at your school respond to conflict. (Scale 1–5) (Factor loadings of .61 or above)

    m. I am frustrated with working with other teachers at school.
    n. I feel burned out at work.
    r. The level of conflict at my school increases my stress level.

DATA ANALYSIS

Qualitative Analysis

Based on Miles and Huberman (1994), the qualitative data were analyzed on three levels. The first level involved preliminary coding. This process aided in the development of descriptive as well as interpretive statements that led to the major findings. Codes are "retrieval and organizing devices that allow the analyst to spot quickly, pull out, then cluster all the segments relating to the particular question, hypothesis, concept or theme" (Miles & Huberman, 1994, p. 56). Some codes were predetermined based on my conceptual model, but I also generated new codes based on the data. This process was necessarily iterative, entailing the generation, revision, and regeneration of codes.

The primary function of these codes was to summarize segments of data. For example, one code originating in the conceptual model was "sources of conflict." Subcodes of these sources included "institutional conflicts," "organizational conflicts," and "individual conflicts."

The second level of analysis included generating pattern codes. Pattern codes are codes that "identify an emergent theme, configuration, or explanation. . . . They are a sort of meta-code" (Miles & Huberman, 1994, p. 69). This level serves a number of purposes, including data reduction, focusing data collection, and "lay[ing] a groundwork for cross-case analysis by surfacing common themes and directional processes" (Miles & Huberman, 1994, p. 69). For example, "conflict-framing" or "conflict ownership" as stances toward conflict emerged as patterns within each school. To help me form these patterns, I wrote brief vignettes. As an analytical tool, a vignette "is a focused description of a series of events taken to be representative, typical, or emblematic in the case you are doing" (Miles & Huberman, 1994, p. 81). This process was helpful in formulating key issues.

For example, I came to see an emerging pattern in teachers at one school, who more often took a multidimensional stance toward framing or identifying conflicts. These teachers identified multiple layers and sources of conflict behind one conflict incident (identifying institutional, organizational, and individual layers to a conflict). I coded this "multidimensional framing."

Another pattern code that emerged was around a school's level of conflict ownership. I came to find that participants at one school tended to publicly identify, openly discuss or debate, and at times eagerly confront one another around issues of difference. I named this "embracing conflict." I also began to realize that the participants in another school tended to end conflict by excluding or marginalizing those considered "resistant," handled differences in private, or transferred conflict management to external authority figures. I called this "avoiding conflict."

Cross-case analysis represented the third level. After Miles and Huberman (1994), I adopted a "mixed strategy" approach to cross-case analysis. In this approach, I wrote up each case and then used matrices and other displays to analyze them. These displays were combined to form a "meta matrix" that I further condensed and compared.

An example of a case matrix involved looking at a conflict incident, the approaches to the conflict, and the subsequent outcomes. Thus, a meta-matrix analyzed the source of a conflict and compared the approaches to, and outcomes of, the conflict using data from both sites.

I used NU*DIST, a software program for analyzing qualitative data, to develop the initial and ongoing codes, locate patterns, and create matrices for the cross-case comparisons. NU*DIST is a flexible tool that allows for recoding, which supports theory generation. With NU*DIST, I developed a data base coding system (identifying school, role of participant, data source) and an analytic coding schema. Developing this schema proved helpful in writing the cross-case analysis.

Survey Analysis

Surveys were analyzed using a statistical package (SPSS). I conducted descriptive statistical analyses (means and frequencies) as well as a T-test to determine statistical significance of specific items across sites. I further disaggregated data by grade level within each school to determine whether there were any differences with the target population that I studied in my qualitative work (eighth-grade teams). I also disaggregated data within the Chavez school by race (Washington had only two teachers of color).

I also conducted exploratory factor analysis to aid in the construction of key concepts in this book, including "embrace conflict," "avoid conflict," "stress," and "teacher learning community" (see Table A.1). Several items from the survey were used to create these factors (see factors and survey

TABLE A.1. *Sample of Descriptive Statistics Comparing Washington and Chavez Middle Schools*

VARIABLE[1]	WASHINGTON SCHOOL MEAN	SD	CHAVEZ SCHOOL MEAN	SD
Embrace Conflict Factor	3.58*	.67	3.06*	.74
Avoid Conflict Factor	2.51*	.68	3.28*	.77
Stress Factor	2.47*	.92	3.22*	1.06
Teacher Learning Community Factor	4.08*	.58	3.16*	.63

*=p≤.05, two tailed test

[1]These scores represent means on a five-point Likert scale where 1 = "strongly disagree" and 5 = "strongly agree."

items in data collection section above). The analysis was used to demonstrate that items in each of these factors measured the same underlying concept. All had a factor loading of at least .62. For all factors, means were created by taking the mean of each survey item and dividing by the number of items. In the case where a teacher did not answer one or more of the items, the average of remaining items was tallied.

I took the means of the items to determine the school's mean score on the factor. Correlations were run between the variables to assess bivariate relationships between them. These data extended my qualitative work and enhanced the coding process.

Member Check

As part of my analysis process I sought feedback from the participants in the study. As Miles and Huberman (1994) explain, "one of the most logical sources of corroboration is the people you have talked with and watched" (p. 275). After I had written a draft of each case chapter I shared it with the school. I held a schoolwide session in which I reported my findings asking for feedback and specifically solicited detailed written comments from a few key informants. I left a number of drafts of the work with the school for teachers to respond to anonymously as well. I felt participants had the right to know how I was interpreting the data and hoped that any findings might help the school in its efforts; thus I made sharing the findings a precondition for access.

References

Achinstein, B. (1997). *Teacher professional community and conflict survey*. Stanford University, Stanford, CA.

Achinstein, B., Meyer, T., & Pesick, S. (1994). Dancing under the umbrella: A story of concurrent, multiple reforms at Cesar Chavez middle school. Unpublished manuscript, Stanford University.

Amason, A. C., & Schweiger, D. M. (1997). The effects of conflict on strategic decision making effectiveness and organizational performance. In C. K. W. De Drue & E. Van De Vliert (Eds.), *Using conflict in organizations* (pp. 101–115). Thousand Oaks, CA: Sage.

Apple, M. W. (1990). *Ideology and curriculum*. (2nd ed.). New York: Routledge.

Argyris, C., & Schön, D. A. (1978). *Organizational learning: A theory of action perspective*. Reading: Addison-Wesley.

Aronowitz, S., & Giroux, H. (1991). *Postmodern education: Political, cultural and social criticism*. Minneapolis: University of Minnesota Press.

Ayers, W. (1993). *To teach: The journey of a teacher*. New York: Teachers College Press.

Ball, S. J. (1987). *The micro-politics of the school: Towards a theory of school organization*. New York: Routledge.

Barth, R. (1990). *Improving schools from within: Teachers, parents, and principals can make the difference*. San Francisco: Jossey-Bass.

Bascia, N. (1994). *Unions in teachers' professional lives: Social, intellectual, and practical concerns*. New York: Teachers College Press.

Bellah, R. N., Madsen, R., Sullivan, W. M., Swidler, A., & Tipton, S. M. (1985). *Habits of the heart: Individualism and commitment in American life*. New York: Harper and Row Publishers.

Bernbaum, G. (1997). *Knowledge and ideology in the sociology of education*. London: Macmillan.

Blase, J. (1991). *The politics of life in schools: Power, conflict, and cooperation*. London: Sage Publications.

Bloom, A. (1987). *The closing of the American mind*. New York: Simon & Schuster.

Bolman, L., & Deal, T. (1984). *Modern approaches to understanding and organizing organizations*. San Francisco and London: Jossey-Bass.

Bridge, K., & Baxter, L. A. (1992). Blended friendships: Friends as work associates. *Western Journal of Communication, 56*, 200–225.

Bryk, A. S., Lee, V. E., & Holland, P. B. (1983). *Catholic schools and the common good*. Cambridge, MA: Harvard University Press.

Burack, C. (1994). *The problem of the passions: Feminism, psychoanalysis, and social theory*. New York: New York University Press.

Calderwood, P. (2000). *Learning community: Finding common ground in difference*. New York: Teachers College Press.

Carnegie Task Force on Teaching as a Profession. (1986). *A nation prepared: Teachers for the 21st century*. New York: Carnegie Corporation.

Chomsky, N. (1989). *Necessary illusions: Thought control in democratic societies*. Boston: South End Press.

Cohen, E. (1990, October). Continuing to cooperate: Prerequisites for persistence. *Phi Delta Kappan*, pp. 134–138.

Cohen, M. D., March, J. G., & Olsen, J. P. (1976). People, problems, solutions and the ambiguity of relevance. In J. G. March & J. P. Olsen (Eds.), *Ambiguity and choice in organizations* (pp. 24–37). Bergen, Norway: Universitetsforlaget.

Coser, L. (1956). *The functions of social conflict*. Glencoe, IL: The Free Press.

Cuban, L. (1984). *How teachers taught: Constancy and change in American classrooms, 1890–1980*. New York: Longman.

Darling-Hammond, L. (1997). Education, equity, and the right to learn. In John Goodlad & Timothy McMannon (Eds.), *The public purpose of education and schooling*. San Francisco: Jossey-Bass.

Deal, T. E., & Kennedy, A. (1982). *Corporate cultures*. Reading, MA: Addison-Wesley.

De Dreu, C. K. W. (1997). Productive conflict: The importance of conflict management and conflict issue. In C. K. W. De Dreu & E. Van De Vliert (Eds.), *Using conflict in organizations* (pp. 9–22). Thousand Oaks, CA: Sage.

Deutsch, M. (1973). *The resolution of conflict*. New Haven, CT: Yale University Press.

Dewey, J. (1916). *Democracy and education*. New York: Free Press.

Etzioni, A. (1993). *The spirit of community: The reinvention of American society*. New York and London: Simon & Schuster.

Felstiner, W., Abel, R., & Sarat, A. (1981). The emergence and transformation of disputes: Naming, blaming, and claiming. *Law and Society Review, 15*, 631–654.

Freire, P. (1983). *Pedagogy of the oppressed* (M. B. Ramos, Trans.). New York: Continuum.

Friedman, M. (1992). Feminism and modern friendship: Dislocating the community. In S. Avireri & A. DeShalit (Eds.), *Communitarianism and individualism* (pp. 101–119). Oxford: Oxford University Press.

Fulbright, J. (1964). Speech to the United States Senate, March 27. Washington, DC.

Fullan, M. (1993). *Change forces: Probing the depths of educational reform*. London, New York, Philadelphia: The Falmer Press.

Fullan, M., & Hargreaves, A. (1991). *What's worth fighting for in your school?* New York: Teachers College Press.

Gardner, J. W. (1991). *Building community*. San Francisco: Independent Sector.

Gerstein, A. (1995). From object to agent: How teachers' roles have changed in two Coalition of Essential Schools member high schools. Unpublished dissertation, Stanford University, Stanford.

Gilligan, Carol. (1982). *In a different voice*. Cambridge, MA, and London: Harvard University Press.

Ginsberg, C. (1994). Killing a Chinese mandarin: The moral implications of distance. *Critical Inquiry, 21* (1), 46–60.

Giroux, H. A. (1983). *Theory and resistance in education: A pedagogy for the opposition.* New York: Bergin & Garvey Publishers, Inc.

Giroux, H. A. (1988). *Teachers as intellectuals: Toward a critical pedagogy of learning.* New York: Bergin & Garvey Publishers, Inc.

Glare, P. E. W. (1990). *The Oxford Latin dictionary.* Oxford: Oxford Clarenden Press.

Goffman, E. (1961). *The characteristics of total institutions.* Paper presented at the Symposium on Preventive and Social Psychiatry, Washington, DC.

Goffman, E. (1974). *Frame analysis: An essay on the organization of experience.* New York: Harper and Row.

Greene, M. (1984). *Education, freedom, and possibility.* Inaugural Lecture as William F. Russell Professor in the Foundations of Education, Teachers College, Columbia University.

Granovetter, M. (1973). The strength of weak ties. *American Journal of Sociology, 78*(6), 1360–1380.

Guiton, G., Oakes, J., Gong, J., Quartz, K. H., Lipton, M., & Balisok, J. (1995). Teaming: Creating small communities of learners in the middle grades. In J. Oakes & K. H. Quartz (Eds.), *Creating new educational communities: Ninety-fourth yearbook of the National Society for the Study of Education, Part I* (pp. 87–107). Chicago: University of Chicago Press.

Gutman, A. (1987). *Democratic education.* Princeton: Princeton University Press.

Hammersley, M. (1984). Staffroom news. In A. Hargreaves & P. Woods (Eds.), *Classrooms and staffrooms: The sociology of teachers and teaching* (pp. 203–214). Milton Keynes: Open University Press.

Hargreaves, A. (1992). Cultures of teaching: A focus for change. In A. Hargreaves & M. Fullan (Eds.), *Understanding teacher development.* New York: Teachers College Press.

Hargreaves, A. (1994). *Changing teachers, changing times.* New York: Teachers College Press.

Hargreaves, A. (1996, April). The emotions of educational change. Paper presented at the Annual Meeting of the American Educational Research Association, New York.

Hargreaves, A. (1997). Cultures of teaching and educational change. In B. Biddle, T. Good, & I. Goodson (Eds.), *International handbook of teachers and teaching.* Boston: Kluwer Academic Publishers.

Hargreaves, A., & Dawe, R. (1990). Paths of professional development: Contrived collegiality, collaborative culture, and the case of peer coaching. *Teaching and Teacher Education, 6,* 227–241.

Hartley, D. (1985). *Understanding the primary school.* London: Croom Helm.

Hirsch, E. D. (1987). *Cultural literacy: What every American needs to know.* Boston: Houghton Mifflin.

Hocker, J., & Wilmot, W. (1985). *Interpersonal conflict.* Dubuque, IA: Wm. C. Brown Publishers.

Huber, G. (1991). Organizational learning: The contributing processes and the literatures. *Organizational Science, 1,* 88–115.

Huberman, M. (1993). The model of the independent artisan in teachers' professional relations. In J. W. Little & M. W. McLaughlin (Eds.), *Teachers' work: Individuals, colleagues, and contexts* (pp. 11–50). New York: Teachers College Press.

Hume, D. (1948). *Moral and political philosophy.* New York: Hafner Publishing Co.

Janis, I. (1972). *Victims of groupthink.* Boston: Houghton Mifflin.

Johnson, D. W., Johnson, R. T., Smith, K., & Tjosvold, D. (1990). Pro, con, and synthesis: Training managers to engage in constructive controversy. In B. Sheppard, M. Brazerman, & R. Lewicki (Eds.), *Research in negotiations in organization* (Vol. 2, pp. 139–174). Greenwich, CT: JAI Press.

Johnson, S. M. (1990). *Teachers at work: Achieving success in our schools.* New York: Basic Books.

Kahne, J. (1996). *Reframing educational policy: Democracy, community, and the individual.* New York: Teachers College Press.

Kanpol, B. (1992). *Towards a theory and practice of teacher cultural politics: Continuing the postmodern debate.* Norwood, NJ: Ablex Publishing Corporation.

Kirp, D. (1982). *Just schools: The idea of racial equality in American schools.* Berkeley: University of California Press.

Kolb, D. M., & Putnam, L. L. (1992). Introduction: The dialectics of disputing. In D. M. Kolb & J. M. Bartunek (Eds.), *Hidden conflict in organization: Uncovering behind-the-scenes disputes* (pp. 1–31). London: Sage.

Levitt, B., & March, J. (1988). Organizational learning. *Annual Review of Sociology, 14,* 319–340.

Lickona, T. (1997). The return of character education. In J. W. Noll (Ed.), *Taking sides: Clashing views on controversial educational issues, ninth edition* (pp. 52–58). Guildford, CT: Dushkin/McGraw-Hill.

Lieberman, A. (Ed.). (1995). *The work of restructuring schools: Building from the ground up.* New York: Teachers College Press.

Lieberman, A., & McLaughlin, M. (1992, May). Networks for change: Powerful and problematic. *Phi Delta Kappan,* pp. 673–677.

Lieberman, A., & Miller, L. (1984). *Teachers, their world, and their work.* Alexandria, VA: Association for Supervision and Curriculum Development.

Lieberman, A., & Miller, L. (1990). Teacher development in professional practice schools. *Teachers College Record, 92,* 105–122.

Lima, J. A. (1998, April). Improving the study of teacher collegiality: Methodological issues. Paper presented at the Annual Meeting of the American Educational Research Association, San Diego.

Little, J. W. (1982). Norms of collegiality and experimentation: Workplace conditions of school success. *American Educational Research Journal, 19*(3), 325–340.

Little, J. W. (1990a). The persistence of privacy: Autonomy and initiative in teachers' professional relations. *Teachers College Record, 91*(4), 509–536.

Little, J. W. (1990b). Teachers as colleagues. In A. Lieberman (Ed.), *Schools as collaborative cultures: Creating the future now* (pp. 165–193). New York: The Falmer Press.

Little, J. W., & McLaughlin, M. W. (Eds.). (1993). *Teachers' work: Individuals, colleagues, and contexts.* New York: Teachers College Press.

Lortie, D. C. (1975). *Schoolteacher: A sociological study.* Chicago: University of Chicago Press.

Louden, W. (1992). Understanding reflection through collaborative research. In A. Hargreaves & M. Fullan (Eds.), *Understanding teacher development* (pp. 178–215). New York: Teachers College Press.

Louis, K. S., & Kruse, S. D. (1995). *Professionalism and community: Perspectives on reforming urban schools.* Thousand Oaks, CA: Corwin Press.

Louis, K. S., Kruse, S. D., & Marks, H. M. (1996). Schoolwide professional community. In F. M. Newmann (Ed.), *Authentic achievement: Restructuring schools for intellectual quality* (pp. 179–203). San Francisco: Jossey-Bass.

Lutz, F. W., & Merz, C. (1992). *The politics of school/community relations.* New York: Teachers College Press.

MacIntyre, A. (1981). *After virtue: A study in moral theory.* Notre Dame, IN: University of Notre Dame Press.

March, J. G., & Olsen, J. P. (1975). The uncertainty of the past: Organizational learning under ambiguity. *European Journal of Political Research, 3,* 147–171.

Martin, J. (1992). *Cultures in organizations: Three perspectives.* New York: Oxford University Press.

McLaughlin, M. W. (1993). What matters most in teachers' workplace context. In J. W. Little & M. W. McLaughlin (Eds.), *Teachers' work: Individuals, colleagues, and contexts* (pp. 79–103). New York: Teachers College Press.

McLaughlin, M. W., & Talbert, J. E. (1993). *Contexts that matter for teaching and learning: Strategic opportunities for meeting the nation's educational goals.* Stanford, CA: Stanford University, Center for Research on the Context of Secondary School Teaching.

McLaughlin, M. W., & Talbert, J. E. (1996). Teacher survey. Stanford, CA: Stanford University, Center for Research on the Context of Secondary School Teaching.

McLaughlin, M. W., & Talbert, J. E. (2001). *Communities of practice and the work of high school teaching.* Chicago: University of Chicago Press.

Merz, C., & Furman, G. (1997). *Community and schools: Promise and paradox.* New York: Teachers College Press.

Meyer, J. W., & Rowan, B. (1977). Institutionalized organizations: Formal structure as myth and ceremony. *American Journal of Sociology, 83,* 340–363.

Miles, M. B., & Huberman, A. M. (1994). *Qualitative data analysis: An expanded sourcebook* (2nd ed.). Thousand Oaks, CA: Sage Publications.

Millet, K. (1970). *Sexual politics.* New York: Avon.

Morgan, J., & Rizzo, L. (1995). *Breaking down the classroom walls: A case study of teaming.* Unpublished manuscript.

Muncey, D., & McQuillan, P. (1993). Preliminary findings from a five-year study of the Coalition of Essential Schools. *Phi Delta Kappan, 74,* 486–489.

Nemeth, C. J. (1989, April). *Minority dissent as a stimulant to group performance.* Invited address to the First Annual Conference on Group Processes and Productivity, Texas A & M University.

Newmann, F. (1994, Spring). School-wide professional community. *Issues in restructuring schools* (Report No. 6), 1–6.

Newmann, F., & Associates. (1996). *Authentic achievement: Restructuring schools for intellectual quality.* San Francisco: Jossey Bass.

Newmann, F., & Oliver, D. W. (1967). Education and community. *Harvard Educational Review, 37*(1), 61–106.

Nias, J. (1985). Reference groups in primary teaching: Talking, listening and identity. In S. J. Ball & I. Goodson (Eds.), *Teachers' lives and careers* (pp. 105–119). London: Falmer Press.

Nias, J. (1987). Learning from difference: A collegial approach to change. In W. J. Smyth (Ed.), *Educating teachers: Changing the nature of pedagogical knowledge* (pp. 137–152). London: Falmer Press.

Nias, J., Southworth, G., & Yeomans, R. (1987). *Primary school staff relationships.* [research in progress] Cambridge: Cambridge Institute of Education.

Nias, J., Southworth, G., & Yeomans, R. (1989). *Staff relationships in the primary school: A study of organizational cultures.* London: Cassell.

Noddings, N. (1989). *Women and evil.* Berkeley: University of California Press.

Noddings, N. (1992). *The challenge to care in schools.* New York: Teachers College Press.

Noddings, N. (1996). On community. *Educational Theory, 46*(3), 245–267.

Peshkin, A. (1986). *God's choice: The total world of a fundamentalist Christian school.* Chicago: The University of Chicago Press.

Pollard, A. (1985). *The social world of the primary school.* London: Cassell.

Purkey, S., & Smith, M. (1983). Effective schools: A review. *Elementary School Journal, 83,* 427–452.

Putnam, R. (2000). *Bowling alone: The collapse and revival of American community.* New York: Simon & Schuster.

Rahim, M. A. (1986). *Managing conflict in organizations.* New York and Philadelphia: Praeger Special Studies—Praeger Scientific.

Rait, E. (1995). Against the current: Organizational learning in schools. In S. B. Bacharach & B. Mundell (Eds.), *Images of schools: Structures and roles in organizational behavior* (pp. 71–107). Thousand Oaks, CA: Sage.

Rosenholtz, S. J. (1989). *Teacher's workplace: The social organization of schools.* New York: Longman.

Rossman, G. B., & Wilson, B. L. (1991). Numbers and words revisited: Being "shamelessly eclectic." *Evaluation Review, 9*(5), 627–643.

Rubin, J. Z., Pruitt, D. G., & Kim, S. H. (1994). *Social conflict: Escalation, stalemate, and settlement.* New York: McGraw-Hill.

Sandel, M. J. (1992). The procedural republic and the unencumbered self. In S. Avireri & A. De-Shalit (Eds.), *Communitarianism and individualism* (pp. 12–28). Oxford: Oxford University Press.

Sandel, M. J. (1982). *Liberalism and the limits of justice.* Cambridge, London and New York: Cambridge University Press.

Schein, E. H. (1985). *Organizational culture and leadership: A dynamic view.* San Francisco: Jossey Bass.

Schön, D. A. (1983). *The reflective practitioner: How professionals think in action.* New York: Basic Books.

Scott, R. W. (1992). *Organizations: Rational, natural, and open systems.* New Jersey: Prentice-Hall.

Scribner, J. P., Cockrell, K. S., Cockrell, D. H., & Valentine, J. W. (1999). Creating professional communities in schools through organizational learning: An evaluation of a school improvement process. *Educational Administration Quarterly, 35*(1), 130–160.

Selznick, P. (1992). *The moral commonwealth: Social theory and the promise of community.* Berkeley: University of California Press.

Sergiovanni, T. J. (1994). *Building community in schools.* San Francisco: Jossey-Bass.

Simmel, G. (1955). *Conflict and the web of group-affiliations* (K. Wolff and R. Bendix, Trans.). New York: The Free Press.

Siskin, L. (1994). *Realms of knowledge: Academic departments in secondary schools.* London: The Falmer Press.

Sizer, T. R. (1984). *Horace's compromise: The dilemma of the American high school.* Boston: Houghton Mifflin.

Smiley, M. (1992). *Moral responsibility and the boundaries of community: Power and accountability from a pragmatic point of view.* Chicago: University of Chicago Press.

Tabachnich, B. R., & Zeichner, K. (1991). *Issues and practices in inquiry-oriented teacher education.* London and New York: The Falmer Press.

Talbert, J., & McLaughlin, M. W. (1994). Teacher professionalism in local school contexts. *American Journal of Education, 102,* 123–153.

Taylor, C. (1992). Atomism. In S. Avireri & A. De-Shalit (Eds.), *Communitarianism and individualism* (pp. 29–50). Oxford: Oxford University Press.

Tjsovold, D. (1982). Effects of the approach to controversy on superiors' incorporation of subordinates' information in decision making. *Journal of Applied Psychology, 67,* 189–193.

Tjosvold, D. (1985). Implications of controversy research for management. *Journal of Management, 11,* 21–37.

Tjosvold, D. (1997). Conflict within interdependence: Its value for productivity and individuality. In C. K. W. De Dreu & E. Van De Vliert (Eds.), *Using conflict in organizations* (pp. 23–77). Thousand Oaks, CA: Sage.

Tjosvold, D., & Deemer, D. K. (1980). Effects of controversy within a cooperative or competitive context on organizational decision-making. *Journal of Applied Psychology, 65,* 590–595.

Tönnies, F. (1963). *Community and society* (C. P. Loomis, Trans.). New York: Harper and Row. (Original work published 1887)

Turner, M. E., & Pratkanis, A. R. (1997). Mitigating groupthink by stimulating constructive conflict. In C. K. W. De Dreu & E. Van De Vliert (Eds.), *Using conflict in organizations* (pp. 53–71). Thousand Oaks, CA: Sage.

Van Maanen, J., & Barley, S. R. (1984). Occupational communities: Culture and control in organizations. *Research in Organizational Behavior, 6,* 287–365.

Wah, L. M. (1994) [Director]. *The color of fear* [Film]. Stir Fry Productions, 470 Third Street, Oakland, CA 94607.

Walton, R. E. (1969). *Interpersonal peacemaking: Confrontations and third party consultation.* Reading, MA: Addison-Wesley.

Weick, K. (1976). Educational organizations as loosely coupled systems. *Administrative Science Quarterly, 21,* 1–19.

Westheimer, J. (1996). Visions of community and education in a diverse society: Essay review of Thomas Sergiovanni's *Building Community in Schools. Harvard Educational Review, 66*(4), 853–857.

Westheimer, J. (1998). *Among schoolteachers: Community, individuality, and ideology in teachers' work.* New York: Teachers College Press.

Woods, P. (1984). The meaning of staffroom humour. In A. Hargreaves & P. Woods (Eds.), *Classrooms and staffrooms: The sociology of teachers and teaching* (pp. 190–202). Milton Keynes: Open University Press.

Yeomans, R. (1985). Are primary teachers primarily people? *Education 13*(2), 6–11.

Yin, R. K. (1989). *Case study research: Design and methods.* Newbury Park, CA: Sage Publications.

Young, I. M. (1990). *Justice and the politics of difference.* Princeton, NJ: Princeton University Press.

Young, I. M. (1995). The ideal of community and the politics of difference. In P. A. Weiss & M. Friedman (Eds.), *Feminism and community* (pp. 233–257). Philadelphia: Temple University Press.

Index

About the Author

Betty Achinstein has worked on teacher development and school reform since 1987, both inside and outside of the classroom. She taught high school in New Jersey and was a founding teacher of an innovative public middle school in Chicago. After completing her Ph.D. in teacher education at Stanford University, she was Director of Member Schools at the Bay Area School Reform Collaborative. Currently Program Director at the New Teacher Center at the University of California, Santa Cruz, Betty is engaged in research, professional development, and policy around quality induction. She teaches about diversity and education at the University of California, Santa Cruz. Her current research and writing focuses on learning communities, teacher development, and teacher leadership.